Memoirs of an Asperger Girl

G000070907

Ducie Hall

chipmunkapublishing
the mental health publisher

Dulcie Hall

Published by
Chipmunkapublishing
PO Box 6872
Brentwood
Essex CM13 1ZT
United Kingdom

http://www.chipmunkapublishing.com

Copyright © Ducie Hall 2011

Edited by Stefanie Kruszyk

Front cover image 'Hollie',
an original artwork by Dulcie Hall

ISBN 978-1-84991-690-5

Chipmunkapublishing gratefully acknowledge the support of Arts Council England.

I would like to give special thanks to my husband for all his patience, my loyal son and daughter and close family friends who have given me their support and advice in completing this book. I am also most grateful to my friends Mr. Stuart and Mrs. Sonia Goodman for their help in completing this manuscript.

Dulcie Hall

CHAPTER ONE
A Child of the Blitz – September 1940

When fishes flew and forests walked
And figs grew upon thorn
Some moment when the moon was blood
Then surely I was born
G. K. Chesterton

A midwife bent over a young woman in labour. 'Push!' she shouted. The patient tried, but nothing happened. 'I'll time these contractions," said the midwife to the patient's mother and she got her watch out and put her hand on her belly. Suddenly a shriek echoed in every corner of the house. 'Another air-raid," the midwife said. 'I'm worried about my mother. I've had to leave her alone.' Marie did not reply as she was more worried about her daughter whose contractions were now getting weaker and weaker. Just then an almighty explosion shook the house. Marie went to the window to see where the bomb had landed.

It was September 1940 and Hitler had now turned his attention to Britain. Against a beautiful blue sky, tiny planes could be seen in dogfights. 'Bang,' another explosion, then more incendiary bombs. 'Look at that,' she said as a plane crashed to the earth in flames. 'One of ours? Or one of theirs?'

Downstairs the midwife set about contacting a doctor. My father was pacing to and fro. He had more to worry about than his wife's confinement. 'As soon as I hear that the Germans are in Maidstone, I'll burn any document we've got that says we belong to a political party,' he said.

As the all-clear sounded, the doctor arrived. 'I will have to do a forceps delivery,' he said. Somehow, they managed to hoist a heavy, tin bath onto the stove and fill it with water. Then the doctor put his instruments into it and told them that the water would have to boil for an hour. Then he'd have to wait for the instruments to cool down before using them.

Suddenly there came the shriek of a whistle 'Another air-raid. Look, I will have to go,' the doctor said. Sometimes doctors had to climb into burning buildings and amputate the limbs of someone trapped by fallen masonry. 'Not much time to give to a woman in labour. I'll come back,' he promised. 'I've heard that Germans dressed as nuns are driving into London,' my father told Marie. 'I've heard that so many dead enemy bodies had been washed up in Pegwell Bay on the night of that storm last week that the locals were saying the Germans attempted an invasion, or possibly a sortie,' he said. 'Let's not pay any attention to rumours.'

Back upstairs they washed the sweat from my mother's fevered brow. Then my father shouted that the water in the baby's bath was now boiling. 'The Germans would surely never succeed in conquering us,' said Marie. 'What about France, a major military power, with the Maginot Line, and the natural defence of high mountains?' Most Europeans had looked up to, even admired France, yet the fighting there had been over in a matter of weeks. Even neutral Holland had succumbed. Suddenly my father rushed out of the front door. Two incendiary bombs had landed in the garden path. Although he was only wearing carpet slippers, Father stamped them out. 'I've heard that policemen are going round lecturing to children at school on what to do should they encounter a German spy.' Everybody laughed but then the midwife said that a man who lived near her had always been taking her niece and other children on little walks. One day the children had come home from school and seen this man handcuffed between two men. It was then revealed that these 'little walks' had always seemed to take place near the airfield. Having children with you would have been perfect cover.

'I'm worried about my three sons at the front' Marie said. 'Preparing for a siege?' Father added. 'So let's buy as much food as possible.' He was collecting a pile of old letters to consign to the flames. Although both my parents were now Christians, my mother had been born a Jewess. Any letter with a reference to this would also have to be burnt. Flames could be seen at the window coming from a nearby house, and smoke could be seen on the horizon. 'They're trying to bomb Woolwich Arsenal,' he thought.

As the all-clear sounded the doctor returned. Everything was ready but the midwife and doctor weren't gaining much success. They kept leaning on my mother's belly to push the baby out, but the doctor said that the baby was caught behind a bone. Eventually he succeeded in carrying out the delivery, and as the baby arrived my mother screamed. The baby girl's head was so badly bruised that they put her aside, not expecting her to live, whilst the doctor got on with stitching the mother. That baby girl was me.

I've been told that I passed all the normal developmental milestones, like sitting-up, crawling and walking, even talking, early. An accelerated growth rate is possible even with autism but when talking for a long time I simply echoed what Mother said. She'd say, 'Where's Daddy,' and I'd say 'Daddy.' Then one day Mum said to me, 'Where's my bag?" and I replied, 'On the table.' After that, I talked normally apart from a tendency to wander from subject to subject.

I'm told that I was an unusually clumsy child and broke something nearly every day. Apparently I broke all the cut-glass vases that Mother had been given as wedding presents. Things just seemed to fall out of my hands. I always seemed to have bags of energy and would run round and round the room banging into everything.

One day my parents couldn't stand it anymore and strapped me into my high chair. I started 'jiggling about' and the high chair promptly turned over with me inside it. (After that my mother wouldn't use a high chair unless it was propped in an alcove.) Then they put me in a low nursing chair and that promptly folded up with me in it too. We had a split-level garden with a rockery in the middle which my father used to jump over. I copied him and fell, cutting my head on a rock. I would wash the last scab from an accident off and fall over again with another nasty graze, sometimes the very same day.

In wartime, when shopping, parents sometimes left children in their prams until they were nearly aged four, so they could get out quickly in the event of an air raid. I can remember throwing blankets out and nearly turning the pram over.

Once I offered to help Mum carry the shopping. 'I'll give you the sugar as you can't break it,' she said. Of course I dropped the sugar and with war-time rationing my mother had to go down on her knees and scrape it off the front step. Clumsiness is a symptom of Asperger's Syndrome, but of course, my parents did not know this.

Once I snatched my father's quinine and drank the entire bottle. I was gasping for breath and my parents really thought they were going to lose me.

I've always been fascinated by trains. Once the police brought me back home having found me sitting on a little stool just outside the station watching the trains go by. I can't remember it, so I could only have been about two.

One sultry August day I saw a little footpath and followed it (my mother had been reading aloud to me), so as I wandered down it, I expected to see little gnomes peeping out from between the bushes. Then I spotted a blackberry and reached up for it, scratching my hand on a bramble. Now I had blood, as well as blackberry juice on my hands, but never mind, I wiped them down the font of my dress. Then I fell into a muddy puddle. I was thinking of A. A. Milne's lines:

> 'I've got boots with grown up laces,
> I know lots of puddly places,
> Who's coming out with me.'

I could hear birdsong and insects droning as I wandered on.

'So there you are. Oh you naughty girl! That dress was clean on today and look at you now. You're getting a good smack when we get home.' I got a lot of smacks, but my parents' anger simply bewildered me. In fact, a tendency to wander away is associated with all forms of autism.

In winter I was the first to feel the cold but in summer I overheated quickly and was always trying to undress. (This too is cerebral.)

Once I ran through the house and threw a duster into the open fire. At that time, with wartime shortages we only had two dusters, so my mother was furious with me. When she looked the other way, I promptly threw the other one in the fire too. I also put a flannel in the bathroom sink and flooded the entire house (my mother thinks I did it more than once). I can remember doing these things, but I couldn't have told anyone why, not even now.

My clearest memories start shortly before my third birthday when an exciting thing happened. My baby brother arrived. He was called Christopher John. This time apparently my mother had an easy birth. But Christopher never stopped crying.

Just after his birth, a homehelp came to take care of me. I became very angry with this person, because she gave me my breakfast and she ate her own food sitting in my mum's chair, but she wasn't my mum.

I had a doll who, to me, was a real person and I invented long imaginary conversations with her. One day Christopher had been put outside to get some fresh air and was crying. Surely my doll would cheer him up, so I went and put her in the pram beside him. Suddenly Mother appeared angry and started shouting at me. I was at a loss to account for her anger but she was later to say that her nerves were worn to a frazzle by Christopher's continual crying.

One night was particularly troubling for Mother. No matter what she did, she couldn't stop Christopher crying. Finally, at about 5.00am, Father got up and took the baby away from Mother and moved him in the carry-cot to the spare room. Perhaps now Mum could get some rest.

The next morning was a beautiful September day. It was my third birthday and Mother planned to give me a big party and had invited a lot of her relatives, as she was going to show off the baby at the same time. She prepared Christopher's bath and feed and took out a special little crème de chine powder blue suit for him to wear. A lot of clothing coupons had been saved up to be able to buy this, as it was going to be a special day. Finally life seemed good again, and Christopher seemed to have settled in the spare room and stopped crying. She was singing as she walked up the stairs to get him.

As soon as she opened the door he was so still that she knew at once he was dead. I was out in the street playing at the time, when the front door of our house burst open and my father came running out with the baby over his shoulder practically galloping to the doctor's house. My mother, also running, was following a long way behind. 'Doctor! Emergency!' Dad shouted as he ran into the surgery pushing past the waiting patients. The doctor tried to resuscitate Christopher but at last he turned to my parents shaking his head. The doctor estimated he had been dead for about 10 minutes.

One of the neighbours in our street saw what had happened and somebody threw an arm round me and said 'Well don't look at it then,' and took me into her house. It seemed like ages before my father came looking for me. He told me that my brother was dead and that mum was getting my party ready. Even then I knew that you can't have a party the day someone dies, but Mother had people coming from the other side of London and nobody was on the phone. She had to clean the house and prepare the food. The food, too, that had been purchased with precious saved-up ration coupons.

The doctor explained to my parents that there would have to be a post-mortem and an inquest, as my brother had not been under a doctor. The post-mortem report, when it came, said that the cause of his death had been inhalation of his own vomit, but this explanation never satisfied my father, who said that this was something they always said at every unexplained cot death.

My parents could not afford a headstone, so Christopher was buried in an unmarked grave with several other cot deaths, or stillborn babies. Any mention of his name would bring my mother out in tears.

Once, Father took me for a walk in the cemetery and became extremely distressed when he couldn't find the grave. He made me say 'poor Christopher' several times and finally when we did find it, we knelt down and said a prayer for him. On reflection I think that Christopher, too, may have been a bit autistic, as the constant crying can be a symptom of this.

Mother said that I asked so many questions as a child that she got to the point where she couldn't stand being alone in the house with me, day after day. So she went back to work, leaving me in a crèche. I'd been there three days when I caught the measles. This was a serious disease before the advent of antibiotics. The week after returning to the crèche I was taken ill again, this time with scarlet fever. After that, my mother decided that I hadn't settled there and quit her job.

Around this time something else happened and I am sure I can remember hearing the name 'Jade' being repeated over and over again. I will come back to her later.

When the Doodlebugs started in the summer of 1944, Mother's nerve completely went. Up till then she'd had a strong feeling that 'it could never happen to her' but now the threat was too close for comfort. Even I can remember the dreadful sound they made. Once, I thought I could hear it again and nearly froze with horror and fear. It turned out to only be a programme about the war on the radio.

'Supposing something should happen to her as well,' Mother thought, looking across at me. So she talked it over with a friend and decided to take me out of London for the remainder of the war and put our names down to be evacuated to the countryside. Her friend, with her small son, decided to come too.

Dulcie Hall

CHAPTER TWO
Evacuation

When my mother put our names down to be evacuated she was filled with trepidation. Everybody was talking about one event so terrible that every single book about the home front mentions it.

Hallsville School in Canning Town was crammed with evacuee families as it was to be the final embarkation point before departure. At about 2.30am that night, when everybody inside was asleep, the Germans flew over and bombed the school. People living nearby said that they saw children's arms and legs go flying into the air without their bodies, in the midst of the smoke and flames.

The repercussions from this event were absolutely enormous. It happened at the weekend so nobody should have been in the school. People said that word had leaked out that the school was full of evacuees and that the Germans had targeted the school deliberately. Buses that should have arrived to take the evacuees away hadn't come as planned. One theory is that they went to Camden Town instead of Canning Town. As late as 1991, notices were placed around the East End saying '50 years since Hallsville School'.

Whatever the truth of it, from then on everything to do with evacuees was shrouded in secrecy.

The evacuation was a big eye-opener for some people in other ways. Most of the people who had offered to take the families in came from the middle classes. Most evacuees, however, came from overcrowded city centres where a lot of people were still very poor.

Some host mothers were horrified when they undressed their evacuee children to find that they had lice, fleas, scabies, impetigo and running sores. Some children had even been sewn into their clothes. Some had no coats and others no shoes. In addition to that, some of the children had never used a proper toilet, seen a knife or fork, or even tasted fresh fruit and vegetables. It had to be explained to the host families that it was not unknown for a family of ten to live in one room with no cooking facilities whatsoever, with a father who'd been out of work for years. In many instances it was a great shock to some families to 'see how the other half lived'.

I was probably lucky to leave with the second or third lot of evacuees. By then it had been decided to have every prospective evacuee undressed and examined by a doctor. I can remember sitting there in my Liberty bodice waiting to have a doctor examine me. They must have been satisfied with me because I was pronounced fit to go.

A few days later, great crowds assembled outside the school where four double-decker buses were waiting. They didn't take us to our nearest station, which would have been Bressington, but instead went to Old Bexley Station via another train line. Once on the train, we didn't go up to Charing Cross or Cannon Street, our normal terminals, but to Victoria Station. There we boarded an underground still with no idea of where we were bound. We passed Paddington, so my mother thought we couldn't be going out West. Finally we all disembarked at Euston and there we learnt our final destination: it was to be the Lake District.

We left the train, I believe, at Kendal and got further buses to, I think, Keswick, although my memory is a bit hazy on this point. By this time it was evening and we all had to sleep in what seemed to me to be a very large room, a church hall I suppose. I remember waking up at night and wanting to go to the toilet and when they finally got me there I couldn't go. Such is childhood.

The next day came what all the evacuees called the 'Slave Market', when locals came round and chose who they would have. Once again, my memory of this is hazy. The Miller family took us. They were Quakers, a banking family from Yorkshire, now retired to the Lake District. Their house, 'Nanny Brow' was on the brow of a hill and was actually a great deal bigger than it looked, and had a good view of Lake Windermere. Mrs Miller, to my childhood eyes, seemed a tall commanding woman. 'You can have the playroom,' she told Mum and I. 'Do you get any air-raids up here?' Mum asked her. 'Yes, they did drop one bomb here,' she said 'It fell in the lake.' I'm afraid we rather laughed at that, after some of the things we'd seen.

It was a great relief to be able to sleep without the constant whine of flying bombs, explosions and the crackle of flames, together with the constant funerals going past in the daytime. Little noises made us jump, and after not having a good night's sleep for years the countryside seemed very quiet.

We had all been on rationed food for years and although this was adequate, it was never so good that you could really enjoy it. The food in the Lake District made us gasp. Milk straight from the cow which was ¾ of a pint cream. Eventually we had to ask for a breakfast between us. 'Nanny Brow' had five bathrooms together with its own land and tennis courts. Once I remember looking out of the window and watching the little red post van making its way up the valley and seeing it turn into our gates. 'That means that someone in this house has a letter,' Mother said. 'Maybe it's from Daddy?'

Then one day it poured with rain and the stream opposite turned into a raging torrent. Mum was taking me out somewhere and the Millers took one look at my little sandals and said 'Get her a pair of clogs!' At that time the poorer people clattered around Ambleside in clogs.

Ambleside was about 1½ miles away but was not on a direct route. Sometimes we were down in the town and thought of getting a bus back. So a bus would draw up, they were all single-deckers in order to get up and down the steep hills. 'Keswick!' the conductor would shout. So people for Keswick would get on. 'Grasmere!' More people, 'Elterwater!' and more would go. 'Sorry lady, we are now full,' so as it was only a walkable distance we would have to walk.

One day I tried to climb onto what looked like a fairly low wall but it fell down and one of the big stones hit my toe. This was my first encounter with a dry stone dyke. I had never seen stone step stiles or post boxes that were built into an already existing wall, being used to the red pillar boxes of home.

Shortly after our arrival, we were told that the Miller's were expecting their children and grandchildren to stay. I can't remember much about the boy, except that he played with model aeroplanes but the little girl, called Hester, I can remember very clearly. To my three-year-old eyes she seemed like a grown-up, but later I realised she could only have been about nine. In her room Hester had a doll that slept in a cot alongside her bed with matching bedclothes to her own bed. My mother also made her some doll clothes. Hester had a doll's house and I can clearly remember her showing me her tiny knives and forks.

'I do hope that little Dulcie isn't bothering you?' Mrs Miller would say. 'Oh no,' Hester replied, 'Dulcie always knocks on the door.' Of course in theory the Millers were glad that I got on with their granddaughter, but in my experience didn't want us to get <u>too</u> friendly.

When people saw that we had bonded with the Millers, they started telling us things. We found out that every week Mrs Miller put ten shillings away for her grandson but never gave the girl anything. Even 60 years later this sort of thing can still make me angry.

I found out that the grown-ups had another meal after I'd gone to bed. One of the maids would sneak me up a little bit of pudding on a saucer. On my fourth birthday I had a party. I can't remember who came to it; the other evacuee children, I should imagine. I was sick, I remember, and they told me 'It's all those little puddings you've been having, after you were supposed to be in bed.'

Once my father came up for a weekend and we went for a trip on lake Windermere. The next day we spent nearly all day walking through the Millers' extensive grounds. We came to little 'Lily Tarn', where all the Millers' water came from. Someone said, maybe it was my father, that the Millers' real decision to take in evacuees was to stop the authorities from requisitioning their house. This did happen to big houses in private hands. Mrs Miller told my mother that she had been prepared to take a woman with two children, but not more. According to my mother, women with say six children received a very rough deal up there, but I knew nothing of this at the time.

One day, Mother and I went for a walk and came to a bridge over a stream. We stood there on the bridge watching the water pass onward to the lake and my mother remarked on how beautiful it all was. Then she read the notice on the bridge and got me, and herself, off it in a hurry. Later my mother told me that the notice had said that the bridge had no foundations or supports and was just balanced finely amongst the rocks.

The Millers' possessed all the latest Dorothy Sayers books. She was a great favourite at the time, and some of her books were set there. Mother was a great reader.

'You go up here and you turn left for Elterwater, straight on for Grasmere,' Mrs Miller would tell us. 'What comes after that?" my mother would ask, and she would reply, 'Nothing.'

Once Mother saw a group of young people out walking and asked them where they were staying and they said 'The Youth Hostel'. It was the first time my mother had ever heard of them.

Finally Mother heard that the Flying Bombs were over. Although rockets had started, my mother thought they weren't nearly as frightening as the Flying Bombs. She missed my father and decided we should return home. Another family, a neighbour of ours, was to travel with us. The day we were due to go home we got a telegram from my father telling us to stay put. 'I know what's happened,' this woman told my mother. 'Your husband's been round to see my husband and he's told him about Hitler's secret weapon.' Nevertheless we went home.

Years later, I was leading a group of young walkers on a weekend at Elterwater, when just by chance I came upon 'Nanny Brow'. It is now a hotel but the little stream that I remember on the other side of the road is still there.

Back home I started at nursery school. At that time they had 60 in a class and yet never complained. When the 'warning' sounded they had to drop everything and get us down the air raid shelter. Once we'd been doing gym, so I raced down there without my shoes being done up and other children were in various stages of undress too. Once down in the air-raid shelter, out came the blackboards, and teaching went on. Imagine today's teachers coping with all the disruption. We were made to drink milk, cod-liver oil and orange juice. It must have meant lots of extra work for the teaching staff.

My next memories were of V.E. day. I can remember the bonfires and the singing. To my great disappointment I had to go to bed. 'Can't I at least stay up till the bonfire goes out?' I begged. Next morning the bonfire was still burning.

Dulcie Hall

CHAPTER THREE
Aunt Jade

From the day of her marriage my mother wanted a child. In 1937 married women didn't go out to work, although a few jobs were reserved for widows. Children came home to dinner and child minders and nurseries simply didn't exist. Every bit of shopping had to be carried home and shopping trolleys, hoovers and fridges were unknown. Also, it could reflect badly on your husband if you worked, particularly if he had a good job.

My parents bought a two-up, two-down, end of terrace in Bressington, Northwest Kent. Shortly after their marriage my father, who was a keen cyclist, organised a cycle ride down to Folkestone where they were to have camped. True, the thought of a pregnancy did just cross Mum's mind, but then her period started.

My father had carefully planned the route. They cycled along the A20 then turned off halfway down Wrotham Hill and cycled along part of the old Pilgrims' Way going down Vigo Hill and crossing the Medway at Aylesford. It would have been about 80 miles but Mum had cycled to Brighton and back in one day before, and she too liked cycling.

They found the camp site but soon after Mother became ill and my father grew frightened. He had a brother that lived nearby and decided to take Mother there and ask if they could stay. In the Thirties, before telephones became widely available, relatives turning up on your doorstep weren't that unusual, and fortunately my uncle was in.

Mother's condition worsened, and my cousin went running down the stairs for my aunt. She in turn became alarmed and called a doctor. In those days people weren't so ready to call a doctor home, particularly as at that time you had to pay.

The doctor told Mum that she was in fact having a miscarriage and was surprised that anyone could have contemplated such a strenuous holiday when pregnant.

Unfortunately it was to prove to be the first of many miscarriages. My poor mother would go to doctors and they would say, 'Oh bad luck, well, try again,' and my mother would get pregnant again and miscarry again. Doctors were respected more then, but also more feared. My father wondered if Mother had strained herself with heavy lifting. He was wrong. When I researched my family I found out that in fact my mother's cervical problems were a sequela from the diphtheria she had contracted as a child.

As Mother kept miscarrying, she decided to go and see a specialist in Harley Street. His fee was three guineas. At that time a man's wages were £3.00 per week, so going to see him was a sacrifice. I don't know the names of every doctor mum saw, but it wasn't very nice. The examinations themselves were painful, but equally hurtful was the attitude of some doctors, one minute examining her, then striding over to wash their hands as if she were something dirty.

Then someone mentioned the gynaecological unit at King's College Hospital in South London and my mother was referred there.

The specialist she saw there in 1939 was called Dr John Peel. 'How many miscarriages have you had?' he asked. 'Five,' Mother replied, explaining that she was being put through an emotional wringer each time she miscarried. 'This,' he said, 'has got to stop.' He advised my mother to use contraceptives for a little while in order to let her body get some rest. Early in 1940 my mother became pregnant again and returned to see Dr Peel, but this time he managed to save me.

Soon after my birth, however, the pattern of miscarriages reappeared and my parents were down at Salisbury at one time, so Mother saw quite an array of doctors, all of whom seemed incompetent.

But nothing illustrates the mistakes that doctors made so much as the case of Aunt Jade.

Early in 1941 my mother's sister, Aunt Jade, came to stay with us. She was the 14th child born to my grandparents. According to my mother, she was an extremely pretty baby, short with a little round face and a mass of red-gold curls. Wherever she went, heads would turn. She and my mother weren't alike or even close, and whatever the circumstances Jade was always cheerful, but lacked mum's intellectual power. Jade wanted very much to be a professional dancer.

While still in her early teens, Jade trained a group of child dancers and went up to the local picture palace and asked to see the manager. There she asked if her group of children could perform at Saturday Morning Pictures, and the manager said yes.

When Jade left school she went after a job in a bookshop. 'Well I don't know about you,' the lady in charge of the shop said. 'You're a bit small, you won't be able to reach the top shelves.' But Jade had caught sight of a small pair of steps round the corner and she went out and came back pushing them. She got the job.

Mother's family was very poor, partly because my grandfather couldn't manage money. His business went bust during the Depression, and he couldn't get a job. He'd been a self-employed tradesman, so he couldn't claim unemployment benefit, or get a pension (the law has been changed on this now). To make matters worse, he went to the pub where he and other ex-soldiers endlessly dissected the battles they'd been in. Mum remembers Jade walking two miles home from work in deep snow. Aunt Beryl says she told Jade to take her wet shoes off, but Aunt Beryl had a reputation for bossiness and Jade wouldn't do it. There was literally no money to feed the younger members of the family.

When the war started, Mum's home broke up. All my uncles were away fighting and my aunts Beryl, Ruby, Sapphire and indeed my own mother were now married. Aunt Beryl's husband found my Aunt Garnet, still then a schoolgirl, a place in a school that had been evacuated to the country. My grandmother, for some reason, went down to the country to live with Aunt Beryl and sold her house or, possibly, had it requisitioned. Jade herself was just at the wrong age. A few years older and she could have joined her older sister Coral in the women's services. A bit younger and she'd have been at school, with possibly free school dinners.

Jade looked round for a live-in job and found one as a mother's help with a certain Mrs Evans. This lady spent all day lying on the sofa. One Monday morning Jade returned late after spending the weekend with my parents. London had been bombed in the night, and fire engines and debris were everywhere, and the buses couldn't get through. Jade was sacked on the spot without being given a chance to explain. So with no job, no money, and nowhere to go, Jade returned to my parents asking if they could give her a temporary home.

Jade was assigned the back room. Mum would hear her up there endlessly practicing her dancing steps. At that time tap-dancing was all the rage and Mum would say that 'she was endlessly jigging about'.

As Father was on essential war work he managed to get Jade a job in his factory. True, Jade had a cough, but like a lot of people who have been semi-starved in their early teens, there was always something wrong with her.

Thinking a bit of exercise and some fresh air would do Jade a bit of good, my parents took her out cycling. Somehow they lost Jade and it later turned out that she had fallen off her bicycle and was badly shaken up.

One day Jade took to her bed and said that she wasn't feeling well. My mother sent up some dinner, but Jade would only eat if Mum took the meal upstairs herself. Later, as a nurse, I saw a lot of this. It's quite common for a desperately sick person to have a favourite nurse and want them for everything. Usually the hospital authorities try to accommodate this as far as possible. Once Dad did take up Jade's tray (after all, my mother had two small children at the time) and Jade wouldn't eat anything, which was a very trying business during the war because of all the food shortages. Then, when Mum went to take her tray, Jade leapt up and grabbed a potato.

All this seemed so odd that my parents took Jade to be seen by a doctor. Jade was frightened of doctors and wouldn't co-operate. She refused to use the spittoon. Finally the doctor said there was nothing wrong with her and she was 'just attention-seeking'. Dad became exasperated with her and it began to cause tension between my parents. I don't know why they didn't try another doctor, but then you had to pay. So Mum wrote to her mother in Salisbury asking if she would have Jade there.

Once down there, Jade found a job with the NAAFI. Did an army doctor pass her as medically fit? Perhaps people piled a lot of the hard work on her because she was willing.

One day Jade was asked to move something heavy, a large cooking pot perhaps, and fainted. The NAAFI staff drove her home and more or less threw her into the house. When Aunt Sapphire found her hours later, Jade was more or less lying at the bottom of the stairs too weak even to reach up and put the light switch on (and she was frightened of the dark).

A doctor sent Jade to hospital, but by this time America had become involved in the war, so she was admitted to a U.S. military hospital. Americans in real life weren't as they were depicted in the movies and Jade could barely understand a word they were saying. They were all in separate rooms, which is usual in American hospitals. Apparently Jade hated it there.

Mum went down to see her and was shown a letter the hospital had sent. She could tell from the way the letter was worded that the whole thing was now very grave. But grandmother didn't seem to take in that things were now very serious and said that Jade would soon be back at the NAAFI, totally cured.

Mum went to the hospital to see Jade for herself. Her sister seemed full of hope, talking about coming over to see my parents with a new green dress that she wished to buy, in spite of clothing coupons and 'teaching little Dulcie to dance'. Still hoping to pursue some kind of stage career, Jade changed her name to 'Jeannette' which seemed more in keeping with her new stage self.

Then Mother went to see the doctor. She was later to tell me that American doctors sat down and talked to you the way English doctors never did. He told mum that Jade had TB and peritonitis. At that time, before the days of antibiotics, the treatment for TB was to collapse one lung. It was too late for this now, because both lungs had become infected and it was now only a question of waiting for her to die. If it had been caught while she still lived with my parents in Bressington, they might have been able to save her. Realising that she would probably never see her sister alive again, Mum asked if she had a favourite food. Jade promptly replied, 'Grapes'.

In spite of wartime rationing, Mum managed to get her some grapes. But by this time Jade was so weak she was only able to eat about two of them. Mum and the rest of the family were told that Jade wouldn't last until Christmas, but Jade complained that no one had bought her any Christmas presents. So Mum bought her a brooch and sent it to her. Towards the end Jade grew so weak she had to call a nurse to turn her over in bed. She passed away on the 17th of January 1942. For the last time nurses washed her beautiful face, now chalky white, that seemed to have dropped in on itself. Nurses combed her (still) long red and gold tresses and laid her out. She had just turned 17.

At the time of her death Jade was still a NAAFI employee, so they paid for her funeral. Wartime Salisbury in January was a difficult place to get to. Trains ran late and petrol was rationed. My mother managed to get to the funeral, but others did not.

Jade's tragic death tore my family apart. Aunt Sapphire more or less accused my mum of murder. Mother burnt her letter and never replied. Personally I think she should have replied, because as it was, the wound festered on. When I went to see my aunt with my second husband, over forty years later, she still seemed to think that my mum was partly to blame for Jade's death.

Father blamed the doctors, firstly the local doctor who had initially examined her, and surely an Army doctor as well. He never really trusted the medical profession again and referred to them from then on as 'tomfool doctors'.

Sometimes my mother would remember people used to make remarks about Jade, like, 'I expect she'll be giving you a lot of trouble with the boys in a few years time.' It's the sort of thing that people used to say about her as she was so pretty. Then Mum would remember that Jade hadn't lived long enough to have any boyfriends and the thought would give her a lot of pain.

Aunt Jade's death led not only to a lot of tension within my mother's family, but also, to some extent, tension between my parents, as they endlessly dissected what they could have done differently. Even I can remember hearing the name 'Jade' being passed back and forth between them both. Jade died when I was two, so they must have gone on talking about it along time afterwards.

It left my parents with a deep distrust of doctors (particularly anything to do with psychiatry) which had a very great bearing on my future.

CHAPTER FOUR
Tara

Mother didn't want me to be the only child, so, as she had been advised, (wrongly as it turned out) that she couldn't have any more children, she decided to adopt. She herself had been brought up by an aunt, and knew the dangers of trying to change a child's inner nature. She knelt and prayed that if the adoption did go through, she would never make a child as unhappy as she herself had been, but would accept it for what was.

In the later part of the war, a baby had been born to a married woman in Brighton whilst her husband, who was not the baby's father, was away fighting. He said he would take his wife back but not the baby, so the baby was offered up for adoption.

I went with my parents to an adoption office in Victoria to collect the baby. We were shown into an upstairs room and whilst we sat waiting, we saw a couple come in with a baby. 'Look,' whispered my mother excitedly, 'I wonder if that's going to be our baby?' The other family were then called into a private room. Soon after that we heard the sounds of a baby crying, followed by footsteps going down the stairs. Finally we were called into that other room and met by an official who quickly put the baby into my mother's arms.

The Adoption Society would never have let us see the other couple if they had been the baby's real parents. It seemed that they had adopted Tara before us, but then the woman found she was going to have a baby of her own and no longer wanted Tara. When my mother got Tara home, she found that all the baby's clothing coupons had been used up, yet the only dress Tara possessed was the one she was wearing, which was far too small and fastened at the back with a large safety pin. At that time, clothes were still being rationed and it seemed as if this woman had used Tara's clothing coupons for her own, forthcoming child. My mother had to go to the welfare for some clothes for Tara.

Mother wasn't too happy about me trying to purloin some of Tara's clothes for my endless collection of dolls. Then Mother found that she, too, was expecting another baby. Was Tara to go back again? 'No,' Mother decided, 'This baby has already had three sets of parents in six months. She's not a doll that we can all hug and pass round. She stays with us.'

When Tara was still a little girl, my mother used to put her out in the back garden to play but instead she would stand by the hedge overlooking the neighbour's garden. The lady next door thought she was looking at her son's toys and pushed some through for her. Finally it dawned on her that what Tara really wanted to do was to play with their little son.

It was at the time of the adoption that something happened that first gave my parents the idea that there might possibly be something wrong with me. We were assigned a social worker to visit us in connection with the adoption. When this person came round, he remarked on the fact that I was a very persistent talker. Some Asperger people are very quiet and withdrawn, but I was the opposite. 'Gabby', some people would say.) The social worker didn't think that Tara and I should be in the same home. Partly because of this, my father decided to take me to see a psychologist. When I was taken in to see this person, I just stood there and screamed and screamed. When this person wrote her report, she said that she wasn't qualified to deal with children. She also said that I appeared to be unusually dependent on my mother and she advised my parents to seek further assistance with me.

Why my parents should take me to see someone who wasn't qualified to deal with children, I just don't know. After their earlier experience with the doctors and Aunt Jade my parents' opinion of the medical profession wasn't very high and they decided to ignore the psychologist's advice and take no further action with regard to me.

Were they right? Everyone told them, 'Don't let the psychiatric people get their hands on you.' Terrible stories were emerging from mental hospitals in the late forties and early fifties. My father was in a position to know more than the average person about what went on in these places because his sister had been a psychiatric nurse. They were frightened that I could be put into a home and perhaps even end up having a brain operation which would definitely have left me a mental defective, and perhaps I would never have been able to leave the place. I've spoken to a psychiatrist about all this recently and asked her if I could indeed have finished up a vegetable in a home for mentally defectives, and she said, 'Those words are truer than you know'.

Rosemary Kennedy, the sister of President Kennedy, was taken into a mental hospital for some apparently trivial reason and given a brain operation which left her a kind of vegetable for the rest of her life. If it could happen to an important person like that, then it could certainly have happened to me. Much later on, I was taken see the plays of Tennessee Williams, where apparently the character 'Heavenly' is based on that of his sister Rose, to whom the same thing happened.

Apparently this person Rose walked around like a complete and utter zombie for the rest of her life.

I suppose if all this had happened today I could have been given a 'statement' for school and it might have saved me from some of the bullying I got at school, if not from the other children certainly from some of the teachers.

After my mother's admission to a home in 2002, when we went through her things, we found some old letters in which she said that she was pleased that Tara and I got on so well together. Unfortunately that isn't the way I remember it. I was born in September 1940 and Tara was born in November 1944 so she was just over 4 years younger than me. When you are a child, four years is a lot. Tara wasn't close enough to me to ever be a playmate, yet not young enough for me to think of her as a baby.

On many occasions when I was playing, I'd look up to see Tara coming for me with, say, a broom, so I'd grab a chair. Then she'd start crying and my Mum would come rushing in and blame me. At that time Tara could only have been about two.

Every time I planned to go anywhere my mother kept up the refrain 'Take Tara'. 'Mum, they're giving away free balloons in the park if you take waste paper up there. Can I go?' 'Yes, but take Tara.' I hated having to have a little sister tagging along, who was soon to be joined by Verity who was born in November 1946, and later by my brother Grant born in December 1947. If I resented having to take Tara everywhere I went, I soon found out that she also resented having to go anywhere with me. The Asperger's Syndrome meant that I was always falling over and this came to be looked upon by my family as a bit of a joke, but it was probably very worrying for people like Tara. Also I couldn't read 'body language' (non-verbal communication) or take up hints and inflections, so I was always misreading people and this was a cause of embarrassment to people like Tara.

Tara had an old doll pram that had originally been mine, and I'd only manage to take my eyes away from her for a minute and she would be off pushing her pram. One time someone took her into the police station. This actually created a problem for us, because the policewomen made a great fuss of her, giving her sweets and so on. So with this treatment, Tara decided she liked being 'lost'. My mother would say to me, 'Where's Tara?' Naturally I didn't know, so my Mum said, 'Perhaps she's gone to the police station again.' So I would have to chase after her and get her back. Once she got as far as the top of the hill and another time she was actually within sight of the police station. Once I got her home and she turned the doll pram round to go back out again, just as I got her to the front door. She could only have been about three.

One day our neighbour hurried over to say that her little boy Trevor, who was about two years old, had disappeared. 'Probably with Tara,' my Mum said, unable to see her either. On this occasion I had not long started school, so Tara would have been well below five, probably about three years old. My mother making me continually take Tara along every time we went to the park meant that Tara knew the way there very well and on this occasion, she'd decided to take the toddler Trevor with her. Finally they reappeared. It seemed they'd been stuck most of the morning in the ladies' lavatory as their little hands hadn't been able to withdraw the bolt. Finally they'd got out by crawling under the door.

I was delighted at the age of seven to be permitted to go on the Sunday school treat, but my father insisted that if I went, then Tara had to go too. He went up there and apparently more or less browbeat the Sunday school into accepting her. Of course Tara hated my being in charge and soon saw her chance to wander away. Someone in one of the other Sunday schools brought her back (at that time they organised a special train with several churches participating) and of course I got into trouble for letting her out of my sight.

Tara liked looking into things to see how they worked, which meant she was always meddling with things and one time she started examining some sharp Gillette razor blades and cut the top of her finger off. Apparently she'd gone into a capillary and worried my mother, who thought the bleeding would never stop.

Once, when I was nearly eight, so Tara must have been nearly four, my father took me back to our original part of London in order to look at some bicycles and for some reason he phoned up my mother at home. Tara had become involved in another accident. My mother had been in the toilet when she'd suddenly heard a terrible scream. Mum raced downstairs thinking Tara had fallen against the electric fire. It seemed that in fact Tara had taken it into her head to machine up a pair of dolls' knickers. She'd been able to get the cupboard door of where Mum stored her sewing machine open and got the thing going somehow. Unfortunately she'd put the machine needle through her thumb. Mum went to the baker next door and he grabbed a chopper and chopped up the sewing machine in order to get my sister away from it. The needle broke up inside Tara's thumb and they took her to a doctor to get the bits of needle out. This had rather a nasty consequence. My father said they hadn't got all the needle out and he held her thumb up to the light and saw the shadow of another piece of needle in there which he finally managed to get out himself on the following Christmas Day. Thank God all this happened before the days of electric sewing machines.

'Tara, you're a meddlesome Mick,' Mum would say to her.

Tara could be a bit deceitful and would do anything to get out of trouble. One day my mother found Verity, crying in the toilet, knickerless and with the floor wet. At first Mother thought that Verity, then only two, had wet herself, but it was Tara's wet knickers that Mother found in the dirty washing. Sure enough Tara was found to be wearing a pair of Verity's knickers. So Tara had wet herself, purloined a pair of Verity's knickers and had shut her in the toilet with its wet floor.

One day we played a game of 'hairdressers' with me as the hairdresser and Tara as the customer. I was in disgrace for ages because I'd cut her hair all different lengths. Shortly after that Tara and I made our own 'tent' in the garden using a clotheshorse and a sheet. Unfortunately we'd chosen one that had been freshly washed.

One day I decided to make-believe I was getting married. I duly hunted around and made myself a veil and headdress out of some of my Mum's net curtains and walked around the streets pushing the latest addition to our family. One or two of the neighbours gave me some very odd looks but I thought it was great. Incidents like this of course partly explain why Tara didn't want to go anywhere with me.

When I got home it was to see a small group of neighbours outside the house gazing up at the upstairs window. First Tara's bare bottom was seen, followed a few minutes later by Verity's. Tara saw me and shouted, 'Hello, we're giving a Punch and Judy show out of the window.' I don't think Mother ever found out about that.

One day Mum found someone's purse in the street and was sorely tempted to keep it as she knew how much Tara wanted a doll. In the end Mother took the purse to the Police Station and the very next day our local postmistress gave Tara a doll.

Tara became very friendly with Roberta Twyford, who lived a few houses along from us. Her father had a wooden leg (a war injury) so he was given a car (and possibly a pension). In the late forties not many people had cars and Roberta's mother used to look very pretty in lipsticks, high heels and jewellery – things my mother could never afford. They often took Tara out. One day I went to an event at the church connected with the Sunday school. It was first event I'd been to in the 'Juniors' as opposed to the primary Sunday school. This would make me 7 or 8, so Tara would have been 3 or 4. When I got home there was a terrible fuss going on, as Tara had not been seen since the morning and they thought she might have come with me. It turned out that in fact she'd been out with the Twyfords who'd taken her somewhere in Essex as they'd crossed Woolwich ferry. It seemed Tara had told the Twyfords that she'd been given permission to go and she'd also told them she'd had her dinner, both of which wasn't true. After that my Dad tried to split Tara and Roberta up. He thought that one's friends should be one's own family. The Twyfords thought that we were too hard on her – she was good at giving people this impression – and they started lying to my parents and telling them that Tara wasn't there when she was. This led to my father going down there and having a big row with them. For years my mother and Mrs. Twyford weren't speaking but Tara and Roberta were soon going round the corner to play.

Grant became very fond of Tara and if Dad was angry with Grant he always went running in tears to Tara. Meanwhile I tended to be the one who took Verity around. One day I was told to take the children up the park whilst my mother 'got on'. By this time we had a younger brother, Clarence, who had been born in 1949, but he was still in a pram at that time. I suppose Tara would have been about five. We had to pass a little park that had an old air-raid shelter which all the local children were using as an unofficial toilet. Tara was going through a stage of using all the 'ladies' in the area and she asked to go so I said yes. When she came out she stayed on the other side of the road and got a bit ahead of me and then waved. Grant promptly tried to run over the road to her and nearly got knocked down by a car. The driver leaned out and gave me what today would be known as a 'mouthful'. Once again I got the blame for it. Tara got told off for it too, but it didn't stop her doing similar things later on.

When Mother gave birth to Clarence, she, like most women at that time, had her baby at home and the council provided a home help service in the immediate fortnight after the birth. However, this person, called Mrs Always, told my mother that with four children under five she could get a permanent home help from the council. So my mum applied and Mrs Always became a regular feature of my life around that time. Mum and Mrs Always would be just about to sit down for their well deserved 'elevenses' when Tara would come in.

'Hello Tara, smell the coffee?'
'Mum, Tom Smith hit me.'
'Well stay inside then. Don't go out.'
'I'll go out Mum, he won't do it again.'

When Tara started school she soon found new strategies for getting her own way. 'Mrs Hewett'—her teacher—'says its a shame that a child of five should only get a shilling as pocket money,' and 'Mrs Hewett says that I need new shoes,' and so on.

When the government decreed that every child should have a daily drink of milk it was unfortunate that they decided to do it through the schools. During the school holiday any child who wanted this milk had to go to the school to get it. Tara put her name down, because her friend liked milk. Mum decided that at five years old Tara was too young to go to school on her own, even though I had been going to school on my own since I was four, and made me go with her. Again this made me resentful because it took such a time out of my day when there were so many things I would rather be doing.

Sometimes Tara's strategies for getting on with people meant that she was able to slide out of trouble but landed me in it though.

When Tara was about six, she saw a girl in the street crying and went over to her to find out what was wrong. It seemed that this girl's boyfriend had just given her up and as Tara seemed so sympathetic, she got out all the jewellery he'd given her and gave it to Tara, saying 'Well it doesn't mean anything to me now.' Amongst the pieces was rather a nice brooch which looked like pale blue china with a girl's figure in colour picked out on it. I won't pretend that it was expensive but I rather liked it and Tara said, 'Well as I've got a lot of other things of hers, I'll let you have it.' So I thanked her and went and put it on my dressing table. I shared my bedroom at that time with both Tara and Verity. Neither Verity nor I got on particularly well with our paternal grandmother but Tara did. Unknown to me and without saying anything

Tara took back this brooch and gave it to our grandmother. The next time Gran came over, she wore the brooch to show Tara how much she appreciated it. I took one look at it and said 'Hey that's mine' and went to take it back. This led to a dreadful row but Gran eventually was allowed to keep it. This episode led to a black mark against me from my Gran.

When Tara was about seven she went through a period of stealing and I seemed to be the person she stole from. She got over it, but it started again when she was much older.

Although Tara enjoyed our Sunday evening sessions of hymn singing round the piano with my Dad, she wasn't really a singer. Although she liked P.T., she didn't really have the strength and stamina to be good at it. She did get things on her school report like 'Tara is helpful around the classroom'.

Tara was not as physically robust as the rest of us and one had only to hear that scarlet fever was around again and she would get it. Whilst hospitalised for this, she picked up chicken pox from another child. Allowed home, Tara promptly gave Verity chicken pox, and she also gave it to Roberta, who she had become friendly with again, in spite of Dad's efforts to part them. Roberta's mother came and asked if Tara could come and play with Roberta as she knew Tara had had it. Of course Tara caught shingles, which is caused by the same virus. If forbidden to go and play in the street, Tara soon found some stratagem for going out there.

It was perhaps inevitable that my parents' idea of entertainment should include lots of walking. When I was aged about twelve (Tara would have been about eight) we went on holiday to a place called Littleham near Exeter. One blistering hot day we decided to walk over to a place called Sandy Bay. On the way back it was noticed that Tara was limping. At the time my parents thought that it was just a combination of hot weather and that she was tired. They rubbed Algipan onto her leg and it appeared to get better. Back home the trouble reoccurred. This time my mother took Tara to be seen by a doctor who then sent her to a consultant. He diagnosed rheumatic fever and advised rest. Tara got no better, so finally the consultant said it was all psychological and that Tara wanted a bit of attention and was trying to get out of going to school. Tara wasn't particularly clever, but she was pretty and popular with the other children and the teachers and my mother knew she had never had any trouble in getting her to go to school before.

So my mother took her to a whole round of doctors. One doctor wanted to start her off on a course of heroin. The doctor had to explain to my parents that she would develop a craving for it and my father got frightened and forbade it. Once again expressions like 'tomfool doctors' seemed to crop up in my father's speech.

Finally Tara was taken to see Dr Sheldon at the Hospital for Sick Children in Great Ormond Street. There Dr Sheldon correctly diagnosed Tara as suffering from Still's disease, a childhood form of rheumatic arthritis.

Shortly after that we read in the paper that Dr Sheldon had been made personal physician to Prince Charles and Princess Anne. 'Well,' Mum said, 'I've reached the top, if he can't help you, 1 can't go much higher.'

When it became obvious that she was going to be in bed for some time, Mum remembered her promise that she would not try and change Tara's inner nature. Tara liked going out and meeting people, so Mother moved her bed downstairs and positioned it so that she could see out of the open window and told her she could have any friend in at any time she wanted. I think this was rather good of my mother because we tended to be a shy, reclusive, stand-offish family.

Tara was eventually prescribed Cortisone, which did in fact help her. When she was able to go about again, my father campaigned to get her a car to take her to school which Kent Education reluctantly, finally provided.

One Christmas some of the teachers put on a pantomime at the school. This took a terrific amount of work and several children helped with writing it. The Arab sheikh was to call out 'Bring on the dancing girls,' and Tara was to come on leading her line of harem girls. (She would have been about nine at that time, as I recall it.) It was very difficult for my parents to obtain the costume, with its saffron-coloured transparent net and elaborate necklace, in which Tara had to do a swaying dance.

Tara was the first to find out that two of the teachers concerned in the pantomime were to be married and also at which local church the ceremony was to take place. She even managed to find out the date and time and she (and half the school) reckoned that they were going up there to see them come out. About two days before the wedding, it was all called off. As they were both very popular, a lot of children had contributed to their intended wedding present and the school had to go back to the bank and get the money back all in the small change that the children had donated it.

Shortly after that the Girl Guides put on a play and this time Tara took the part of a Victorian girl in a long white gown. She did in fact look very good in it and the harem girl costume.

When I was about fourteen I decided to become a writer and was sitting in the front room trying to write stories. I was bent over concentrating really hard when suddenly Tara came in – she would have been about ten at that time – and started making faces and generally trying to annoy me (wind me up as they would say today). I thought, 'Well, I give up,' and grabbed everything, fountain pen, ink, exercise book and everything else I was using – at that time we used fluid ink – and rushed upstairs and went to my room where I went on writing. A few minutes later Dad came to tell me that there was ink on the stairs and that I was to blame. I never found out whether Tara deliberately spilt the ink to get me into trouble or whether I, with my clumsiness and desire to get away from her, had done it by accident. I do know that he blamed me and kept on bringing it up years and years afterwards whenever we argued about anything, as we did in my teens.

When Tara was about twelve, she was the first to come home with the news that one of our neighbours was drinking heavily. Soon, however it became common knowledge and we had to have their little son over at our place because his father was too drunk and violent for him to return home.

As Tara was only 4'10" and I was 5'10" and a completely different colouring to her we were never able to have the long 'girlie' talks about make-up and clothes that some sisters have and of course we could never, ever wear each others' clothes. Tara was the first one of us to become interested in clothes and with her small, neat figure, trousers suited her very much. She couldn't have been much more than about twelve when Mother saw her and her friend whispering outside a house a few yards down the road. 'Who lives there?' Mum asked Tara, and she blushed. So Mum thought, 'It's one of those sort of friendships, is it?' By sixteen or seventeen

Tara was courting seriously and at eighteen became engaged, although she didn't get married straight away because he was away in the army.

She made a beautiful and radiant, young bride. As soon as she married she moved into army accommodation and after that we only saw her intermittently.

Once when I went over to see her, I noticed she didn't look well and so I asked her what the matter was and she said, 'My old trouble.' So to me it doesn't sound as if her illness could even remotely have been psychological in origin. I don't see very much of her now, although I've heard she's managed to regain contact with her original family. People talk to me about 'regaining your former closeness' but as I don't remember ever being close to her, it doesn't seem worth it.

The way the hospital let her catch chicken pox when she'd gone in there with scarlet fever and was being nursed supposedly, in a fever ward, hardly inspired confidence. Then they failed to see that she still had part of the needle left inside her finger. Then her Still's disease was misdiagnosed as Rheumatic fever. I also have never, in 10 years of nursing, heard of anyone else being prescribed a dangerous drug like heroin for rheumatism. There was nothing much to inspire confidence in the medical system generally, particularly psychiatry. All this of course had a bearing on my own future.

Perhaps the best thing that I can say about Tara is that although we've never been close, she's just about the only member of my family that I'd ever feel able to trust with a secret.

Dulcie Hall

CHAPTER FIVE
Bernard Patton

A short time after we moved to St. Sadie's Park a classmate, Leticia, asked me to go to an evangelical Sunday school with her. When she assured my parents that there were no busy roads to cross, they said that I could, and later they themselves started attending the little chapel, though not regularly.

There were allotments which backed onto the chapel and we used to surreptitiously creep in and help ourselves to great long sticks of raw rhubarb.

I always enjoyed the religious services. I loved the singing and the power of the words, 'God is still on the throne, and He will remember His own.'

In those days thousands of children attended Sunday school. I've often wondered why that was. Perhaps it was because hardly anything else was open, the petrol rationing and little traffic? But that was only part of the reason. It was largely something psychological about the fact that we were still, in 1946, living in the shadow of the war. When the elevator goes down the lift shaft the weight comes up. Perhaps it was all a reaction to the fact that we'd just defeated the godless hordes of Nazism. There were worries about whether Hitler really was dead, atom bombs, and traitors that were round every corner. Food and clothing was still rationed and even china and saucepans were difficult to get. Troubles all round, and people wanted to know that God was still on the throne.

As we drew away from the war it slowly became known that 'our boys' hadn't always behaved like plaster saints either. I remember one airman who'd bombed Hamburg saying that he reckoned he could smell dead bodies from the air. People who felt guilty wanted to know that they'd been 'ransomed, healed, restored, and forgiven,' as the old hymn says.

Once the children at the chapel performed an allegorical play in which two cardboard giants named 'Greed' and 'Self' were carried onto the stage. One of these giants looked suspiciously like Hitler.

The chapel services had about six very bright hymns per service and the Lord's Prayer was also sung. Pastor Goode would read from a psalm, 'Who is This King of Glory?' and we would reply with the next verse, 'The Lord of Hosts, He is the King of Glory,' and so on.

In every chapel there is usually a hard core of two or three families who keep it all going. In this particular chapel one of these families were the Uptons. Every Sunday half way through the service the minister, called upon the steward to read the notices, and Mr Upton, a stooped, seventy-year old, would slowly make his way to the front. He would peer at the bits of paper and rummage through them. Finally he would say, 'There will be a ramble for the young people on the forthcoming bank holiday.' Rummaging again through his notes, he would continue, 'Choir practice on Friday evening.' If you were sitting more than four pews from the front you couldn't hear him anyway. Everybody knew that now that Mr. Upton's sight and hearing had deteriorated he should give up the job of steward, but as soon as it was suggested that someone tell him everyone said 'not me'. It was Mr Upton's job and he had been doing it for years and didn't see why he should give up 'the Lord's work'.

Every Sunday before the service a little side door would open and out would file the seven deacons who would take their place in the congregation. One of the deacons was a man named Bernard Patton, who was also the

Sunday school superintendant. His wife Penelope was head of the Primary Sunday school. I liked this couple very much. While I was a 'primary' child, the Asperger's Syndrome that I suffered from made me into an 'awkward' child, if not rather a lonesome one. But Penelope Patton seemed to have just the right, deft touch with me. She had a tall, commanding figure and could be in turn motherly with the little ones, yet firm. Bernard Patton was a self employed lawyer and was (by my parents' standards) well off. He had a son called Maurice and they had adopted a little girl called Marilyn, who would have been a couple of years younger than me. As she became quite friendly with my sister, Tara, I got to know her quite well. Sometimes my father made toffee apples and then Marilyn would come round. Maurice often cycled round to call her home.

Once we heard that the circus had come to town and were planning as a publicity stunt to march their party of baby elephants round the town. They were due to pass the chapel during Sunday school time. When we arrived, Mr Patton told us that he had heard about the elephants and they were planning to stop everything so that we could go out and see them. Something must have gone wrong somewhere, though, because we missed them.

I can remember a family named Grafton. Apparently their parents planned to have 12 sons and name each of them after one of our Lord's disciples. Her first son was duly named John, but after that the powers that be would only grant her girls and they duly became Andrea, Simone and Petra. 'Good job she didn't get as far as Bartholomew or Nathaniel,' someone remarked. Everyone knew that John was really the family favourite. The Grafton family said prayers every morning and evening. Mrs Grafton once told my mother that her husband handed her his entire wage packet unopened and she gave him back a certain amount every day for pocket money. John had barely reached 12 years when Mrs Grafton began looking round for a future wife for him. Her eye lighted on Zoe Clayton, so she encouraged Zoe to her home, and got very excited when Zoe started using make up.

Everybody looked forward to the Sunday school treat. In my first year we simply went to Chessington Zoo (now Chessington World of Adventures) but every summer after that we went to Westgate. Together with several other Sunday schools in the area, the Pattons had hired a special train.

The things that we children got up to on that special train! Before we reached Gravesend the train passed some kind of canal and there was a lot of water. Then, when the train clanked over an iron bridge, we all craned out of the window to see who could be the first to spot Rochester Castle. Then we would see the lights come on. 'Tunnels!' we would yell as the train went under the North Downs. 'Whoooooeeee!!' One year the lights did not come on. I can remember Leticia hanging out of the window trying to catch streamers. John Grafton, leading others, climbing on the luggage rack. Eileen and others decided to play 'Consequences'. You wrote the name of someone fairly well known and then passed the papers on. Then we would write 'met', then we would think of another famous name. Here we passed the papers on again and tried to think of some unlikely place where they could have met. Then we wrote that down and passed the papers on again and eventually we would take it in turns to read them out. Simone might read something like, 'Danny Kaye met Bessie Braddock in the Ladies Lavatory.' Someone decided that this game really was just a little bit sinful. So we pulled all the blinds down and went on playing it.

As the train neared Whitstable, we would all hang out of the window, trying to be the first to spot the sea.

At Westgate we had our picnic on the beach. Then we would go in the sea, or we might perhaps build a truly magnificent sand castle. Once Mrs Patton brought a spare pair of knickers for a girl whose parents couldn't afford a bathing costume. We might even walk right through the water to Margate, where we visited 'Dreamland', a large fun fair on the front. There we could go on the Big Dipper or the Ghost Train or the Scenic Railway. Or we could go and see the girl in the pit with the crocodiles, who really was a bored girl pushing baby crocodiles away with her foot. We weren't always able to go away every year, so this was exciting.

When summer came to an end, we would have the truly magnificent Harvest Festival service to which we all took gifts of food. I can still remember the beautifully decorated church, and the smell of apples.

Every Christmas we had a children's party and somebody would always dress up as Father Christmas and distribute presents. I would be sitting next to Marilyn, and as Father Christmas entered, she would say excitedly, 'Its my Daddy, I know its my Daddy.' We had all recognised his voice. On the way to Sunday school we would see his 10-seater car go past and it was always full of children, but Bernard Patton always managed to wave to us. At that time not many people had cars, so he was always ferrying someone around. We would all do what was then called a 'Buzz Up': folding our arms across each other's bodies at the back. We would sing, 'He rolled back the waters of the mighty red sea', sway to the right, followed by, 'He said I'll never leave you if you put your trust in me," and sway to the left, or, 'Behold I stand, I stand at the door and knock,' and we would all bang on the floor with our feet, all trying to outdo each other with our knocks.

I can see Mr Patton today with his round, chubby face. He was a great soul to have around whenever you had a party (church socials). He always seemed to have a cheery word for everyone and he never let anyone feel left out. Not only did he get on with the younger children, but the young people in the youth club adored him too. He was all things to everybody, and there is an art in doing that.

In addition to running the entire Sunday school between them, the Pattons also ran the youth group. Once the Pattons taught everyone to make raffia baskets. 'We think that the young people are better actually doing something,' Penelope told my mother.

Eileen's mother made her and her brother a dress and a shirt out of an old silk map. I marvelled at this, as my mother couldn't have done anything like that. Then Eileen's mother died unexpectedly and she had to be the 'mini-mum' for her little brothers. When Leticia failed the 11+ her parents decided to send her to a convent school and thought it would be easier for everyone if Leticia became a Catholic. Her friend Candida, who always copied Leticia, left with her.

I can remember discussing current events with Mr Patton, like 'Acid Bath Haig', the Korean War and the Queen's Coronation.

When I was about twelve, they formed a break in the Sunday school and split it into two groups and Mr Patton was put in charge of the older half. My chief memories are of coming home from morning service and smelling the roast lamb cooking and listening to Jean Metcalfe with 'Two Way Family Favourites' on the radio.

At that time the Sunday School Union used to organise something called the Scripture Exam, which we all duly took. In addition to the Scripture Union prize Mr Patton used to award a prize, paid for by himself, to the top student in our Sunday school. All the prize-winners were called out to the front and received their prize from the rostrum. One year both myself and Tara were in the running for an attendance prize as we had attended on all 52 Sundays. 'No one can beat that,' I thought, but I was wrong – it had been a leap year, and John Grafton had been there on all 53 Sundays. The results of the scripture exam were even published in a local paper.

When Marilyn was about 10 years old, the Pattons took her to a child guidance clinic because her mother had complained about her continually fidgeting. The child guidance people had suggested that she might be better off in boarding school. Apparently Bernard Patton had to call at the school every Wednesday to collect whatever Marilyn had cooked that day. Once, when I was on a trip to London, I saw a 'crocodile' of children approaching and I suddenly realised that someone was waving madly to me. Then I saw that it was Marilyn. No-one was ever going to turn Marilyn into an intellectual, but she was a pleasant young girl, happy enough and liked by most.

Attending Sunday school was always a happy occasion for me. I always saw Christmas as dark, velvety red. Easter was a bright yellow, Whitsun (for some reason) was light blue. Harvest Festival was a rich yellowish brown. The chapel was saving like mad for a new Hall and kept holding bazaars to raise the necessary money. In addition to that, everyone gave to Foreign Missions, and this particular chapel had various links with Sri

Lanka as Rev. Good, our pastor, had been a missionary in Sri Lanka before his appointment to this position.

On a couple of occasions I had to go to the Patton family home. They had a massive corner property with stained glass windows, and a door bell that sounded like a series of chimes, which was very much an innovation back then. I often thought how very lucky Marilyn was. (Maurice, too, was being privately educated.) Her parents had money, but more importantly she had a father she obviously adored.

Chapelgoers tend to be very interested in the Old Testament, and one day Rev. Good preached a sermon on the Prophet Elijah's curing the Syrian Naaman of leprosy. He invited all the young people to write him an essay on it. The winning essay was to receive a prize awarded by him. Then someone offered a second prize. Apparently he only got three entries so he appealed from the pulpit for someone to award the third entrant a prize. He said, 'I know someone will.'

Then Maurice got a brain tumour and died very suddenly. He was only 15 years old. We heard that the shock had sent Penelope Patton blind. (She hadn't told anybody about this, but apparently she had lost the sight in one eye when she had Maurice.) The Sunday when Rev. Good was to have awarded the prizes came and went without him mentioning the prizes. Then, when I got home, my parents asked me when I had last seen Mr Patton.

I told him that I had been walking up the drive in front of the church with Eileen when we'd seen Mr Patton ahead and whistled to him. He was the kind of adult who you knew would just laugh that kind of thing off, without running to your parents with tales. He would have simply turned round with some cheery word. Then my father said, 'Well, we've heard that he's left his wife.' At first people were so shocked that they just didn't believe it. At that time we didn't know anyone who was separated, let alone divorced.

One day I was late in going to church and I saw that Mr Patton had parked his car right in front of the chapel and had started cleaning it while the service was going on. Was this why no-one had mentioned the Naaman prize? Was Mr Patton supposed to have paid for one? We were told that Mr. Patton had gone off with a woman who had seven children, and that the husband she had left had gone insane. He was taken to a mental hospital and I don't know if he ever came out, but I know their house stood empty for years.

Bernard Patton must have loved children and desperately wanted some of his own. Perhaps he hoped that this woman, whom we will call Jane, with all those children would be able to provide him with a son to replace Maurice. Or maybe he just couldn't cope with a handicapped wife.

Marilyn, who had by this time returned home, was absolutely distraught by the loss of her father – she had to read aloud to her mother the note that her father had left – and there were tales of her being seen stealing from the collection plate.

My mother suggested that some of us ought to go round to visit them and offer to read some of the sympathetic letters that surely must have arrived, but my father said no. He said that as they were very well known people, many, many more people would have offered.

What could one do that would possibly help Penelope Patton? I thought of reminding her that Fanny Crosby, who wrote the hymn 'Blessed Assurance', was blind, but

Fanny's husband had stood by her. Another blind hymn writer was George Matteson, whose fiancée had broken it off when she knew what was going to happen to him. It may have helped Penelope to realise that other people had been there before her, but it could simply have reinforced her own pain and hurt, so I crossed it out. Then I thought of writing a note to her that would say, 'We're praying for you,' but somehow that didn't sound right either.

What I should have done was just go up to Penelope and take her in my arms, and say how sorry I was. At 13, I wasn't quite up to doing this – my own family had never gone in for hugs and kisses anyway – and in any case, Penelope never invited sympathy. I kept trying to think of something that would help Penelope in some way, and but couldn't think of anything. I can remember seeing her stumbling along with her white stick, thinking that after practically running the church for years and years, it must have been hell for her to know that people were now feeling sorry for her. Of course I had no idea what was wrong with me at the time, but I was beginning to realise, albeit only dimly, that I had a severely limited personality. I felt guilty, feeling that I'd taken a lot and given nothing.

I've realised since that it wasn't just after it happened when Penelope Patton needed the help, but a couple of years afterwards, when everybody was used to her being a blind, single mum. I had to go round there again a few years later and by this time their home was looking a trifle dilapidated. The lawns, obviously, now wanted cutting. Marilyn was to tell me that they couldn't get anyone to do it.

Some years later Penelope moved out of her home into a little flat just opposite the chapel. She told my Mum that everybody had told her that she would regret leaving her home, but in fact so many bad things had happened there, that when she turned the lock in the door for the last time, all she could feel was relief.

Meanwhile Marilyn grew up. After various jobs she got a job as a nurse away from home. I spoke to Penelope and she said that she was thinking of selling up and going to join her, since, as she put it, 'Marilyn is all I've got now'. I asked what would happen if Marilyn got married, but Penelope said that Marilyn was now nearly thirty and she had never had a boyfriend.

About 10 years after Bernard Patton left his wife we heard that he had been hospitalised with a heart attack. Marilyn rang this person, Jane, to find out how her father was, but all Jane would say was, 'I don't know why you are so interested because, as an adopted child you weren't really his daughter anyway.' Suddenly Marilyn seemed a lot more mature.

Then Marilyn was back home again and now engaged. Her fiancé was Greek and Penelope told us that his family wanted a fairly big wedding. After Mr Patton died everything went to Penelope, who was still his legal wife. Penelope gave the house that Bernard and Jane had been living in to Marilyn and her husband as a wedding present. Marilyn can't have been expecting to get it, because I'd seen her only a few days before and she had been talking about buying a house.

I dreamt about Bernard Patton recently and woke up thinking that everything would be alright now he was in charge. Then I remembered that he was a man who had deserted his disabled wife, in what must surely have been the hour of her greatest need. I've seen some nasty betrayals since, but somehow you always remember the first one.

Shortly after my second marriage, when I was visiting my parents, I asked after Penelope Patton, to be told that she had died some two years before.

I left the little chapel shortly after Mr Patton's defection. I can't ever remember the Pattons ticking me off, but after he'd gone I always seemed to be in hot water over something. The man who took over his job – hurriedly, without anything much prepared, as I've realised since -- didn't seem a patch on him. Everybody I knew were now scattering, either marrying or emigrating. Suddenly the Evangelical sect which I'd grown up with seemed a little bit confining and I wanted to know what else the world had to offer.

Over fifty years have gone by since Mr Patton's defection. Thinking it over, I now think that we were too reliant on another human being when, as a Christian, I should have put my faith only in God.

CHAPTER SIX
Father

My first memory of my father was being taken to see the Bertram Mills Circus at Olympia. They had dogs dressed as little girls walking on their hind feet. Next came the trapeze artists. Suddenly the audience gasped and stood up, seeing someone fall into the safety net, but it was only a long cloak that had been dropped, maybe deliberately.

Because of the war, the firm Dad worked for had to go over to making part of the fire power for a ship. One day, half of St Mary Cray village was bombed. Dad spent a whole afternoon trying to comfort a member of his staff who had lost both her parents, wondering uneasily whether it was the huge railway viaduct which crossed the village or the factory that had been the real target.

Every Friday I would go to meet my father from work with my sweet coupons. Aged only seven, I was pleased to be trusted to take two buses on my own. Dad always said that if you wanted sweets, go to a proper sweet shop, not a newsagent, and get them to weigh the sweets in front of you. He'd found a tiny, dimly lit sweet shop in Footscray. It smelt of spicy sugar and chocolate ginger, and to me was like an Aladdin's cave. You could see the dim gleam of huge jars of brightly coloured sweets piled high on shelves. Dad wouldn't buy milk chocolate. He said that this was a war-time idea to cheapen it. He preferred bitter chocolate, which was what he claimed lifeboats always carried. He bought dolly mixtures, smarties and liquorice allsorts for us and Pontefract Cakes or Hacks for himself. He always bought cream soda, lemonade, ginger beer or Stone's Green Ginger Wine, a mild alcoholic drink suitable for children. At that time, shops kept special tidbits for their regular customer.

At home I would sort the liquorice allsorts into piles according to colour and shape, then spread them on my bread.

Although Dad liked the odd glass of beer, such as stout or shandy for Sunday lunch, he didn't like going to pubs, saying that the smoky atmosphere in pubs made his hay fever and asthma worse. He often gave us a tiny glass of mild wine or a small taste of beer. He thought that if children learned to drink at home under their parents' supervision, they rarely became alcoholics later.

Dad never liked lewd jokes and he never took my mother's arm in public. As children we were never hugged or kissed as he considered that kind of behaviour a bit 'soft'. In fact he said that some parents did that sort of thing to cover up over how little they thought of their children.

Dad loved music and had taught himself to play the piano. He also had an old harmonium with only one pedal. He played light classical music, usually Elgar, Gilbert & Sullivan or the musical version of the 'Pied Piper'. He also played and sang the popular songs of his day. On Sunday evenings we often had a long hymn, or carol singing session around the organ. We'd sing through something we'd heard in school assembly or our singing lessons, and he could always play it straightaway without music.

At local dances (usually given by the Co-operative Society) Dad was always one of the first to take to the dance floor. He liked things like the 'Dashing White Sergeant', or the 'St. Bernard's Waltz'. In fact he actually organised and was MC at a Dinner and Dance at his place of work. He couldn't stand the discotheques that came later.

One time a pair of actors came down from London's West End and opened what was a 'little theatre' backing onto their own, quite large home. There they performed pantomimes at Christmas and also ran dancing classes for children who would later appear in their shows. Dad knew these people and I think one of the reasons my parents bought our house was because we would be near to this theatre crowd. My Dad was very keen to enrol me for the dancing classes that they ran.

I was tall and heavy for my age and had little sense of rhythm. Later I was to find out that I had one leg shorter than the other, dropped arches and badly misshapen feet. However, the real reason why I didn't have much idea of how to dance was because the autism I suffered from, which made me very clumsy. I practically tripped over my own feet. In fact, I was more equipped to be a one-girl crazy gang show than ever flit around the stage like a delicate fairy.

After a few weeks passed, I was politely asked to leave. My father was bitterly disappointed as, apparently, he'd gone to some considerable trouble to get me in there.

As he had only taught himself to play the piano by ear, he wanted me, the eldest, to be formally taught the piano. I wouldn't go to the lessons, so some time afterwards he bought me a recorder, but I gave it up after only a few lessons.

Looking back I suppose my father thought he was offering me the musical chances he hadn't had and the fact that I couldn't really do it was, I think, the first point in the estrangement that was later to arise between us.

When I was eight years old, we went on holiday to Rhyl in North Wales. It was bitterly cold for most of the holiday, but waiting at Rhyl station on the way back it turned very hot and I became very thirsty. (This again could be cerebral; I have always re-acted very quickly to extremes of heat and cold). I tried to wander off and get some fruit (this was before the days of buffet cars). My mother promptly asked where I was going. 'Let Daddy go,' she said so I duly handed the money to him. A few minutes later he came back: 'Look, I couldn't get you any fruit so I bought sweets instead.' To be given sweets when you're thirsty only makes matters worse.

On this occasion he also bought a large bouncy ball which I took to school with me for some time. One day I was throwing it around in the kitchen, when it landed on top of a very high cupboard, where it lodged itself behind a lot of other occasional kitchenware that had been placed there to be out of the children's way. Getting it down would have meant a ladder and sorting through various items, so my mother put me off and said that they would get it down 'some time'. I never forgot that my ball was still out of reach and in fact, as I remember, it was about two years later that the cupboard was finally cleaned off – a major undertaking at that time – and my ball was found, at which point Verity promptly claimed it was hers, and without any reference to me my father just gave it to her.

My father could mend anything, and once he came across a discarded old steel foot. He stayed up till late in the night using it to mend all our shoes. He was also, when he put his mind to it, a very good cook and he washed up too, saying the steam helped his asthma.

One day, around the time I was nine, my family decided we should play a game of Ludo and my parents started the game off. They shook the dice, got their sixes, and within the first few moves it became evident that Dad was going to be the winner. Finally I got a six and started my game way behind the others. This game had a 'go-back clause' which meant that at one point Father had to start all over again. This turned the tables somewhat and this time it actually began to look as if although I'd started last, I might, after all, be going to win. Then my father threw an entire row of sixes and started to laugh uproariously as he put his tongue out and divided the board up into various lots, i.e. three here, nine there and proceeded to knock all my counters off the board in the process. I started to cry and my mother spoke to him and he finally he allowed my counters back on the board again. I don't know why he didn't want me to win or, to put it another way, why he was so keen to beat me and cause me distress. Ludo is completely a game of chance. As an adult I have discussed this incident with other people, and no one can see why I was so upset over it. A friend of mine, who has helped me understand a lot of these perplexing experiences, simply laughed when I told her and remarked that men have very fragile egos and when they played chess with her father, they always had to let him win. My own mother urged me to 'grow a thick skin. Most men are much the same. You have to learn to laugh things like that off.' Of course, it was my mental condition that made me smart so much over things like that. To me it didn't seem worthwhile playing if I knew who had to win. After that whatever game he suggested I made some excuse.

Now, I tend to think he was playing some kind of game with me. Every schoolboy bully does it: if they know they can wind you up, they do it all the more.

In fact the days of families sitting and playing cards in the evening were nearly over, as radios and then TV were about to burst on the scene.

As chapel-goers we weren't allowed to do much on a Sunday. However my parents were keen cyclists and so on Sunday afternoon we would go out on their tandem. Tara would sit on a special saddle between the handlebars, and Verity and Grant would go in the sidecar whilst I rode my fairy cycle beside them. That way we were able to explore a little of what went on in the woods around St. Sadie's Park. Once we heard the first cuckoo.

Dad didn't like us going to the visiting fair on bank holidays. He would say, 'They always put the prices up then.' He also didn't like us buying flowers for Mother's Day, saying it was 'an American idea, just when flowers were at their most expensive.' Saturday morning pictures were out of the question. Sometimes we were able to persuade him that a certain film had educational value. That way we got to see some films such as 'Hamlet', 'Little Women', and 'Mandy'. But we weren't successful with Oliver Twist or with one I very much wanted to see, 'Father Brown', as it was given an 'A' certificate.

When 'Julius Caesar' came out, however, Dad decided to go and see it himself. He cycled down to the Odeon on the tandem, forgetting that it would be dark when he came out, and the bike had no lights so he would ride it home through the woods. On one occasion, only too conscious that he shouldn't be riding it, he started scooting the tandem. Just at the end of our road he ran into a policeman, who promptly nabbed him, thinking that because of his guilty air, Dad had stolen the tandem. 'What breed of bicycle is it?' the policeman wanted to know, but Dad had bought it second hand years before, and had no idea what make the cycle was. 'Well my mates at work call it the Flying Bedstead,' he ventured at last and the policeman let him go.

As a youth, my father had never been attached to any particular church but liked to go anywhere where he heard that someone interesting was preaching, such as when he heard the Rev. Dinsdale Young. He also claimed to have heard Charles Spurgeon preach, but the dates don't quite seem to fit.

Father once pointed out the former home of the explorer Shackleton, with whom he had a vague connection. Apparently Shackleton toured round giving talks to schools to raise money for his expeditions and might have given a talk at Father's school, but once again, I can't quite match the dates.

Father's family originated from Bermondsey in inner London and had worked in the docks as sailmakers. He had two maiden aunts who had worked in a Bermondsey sweet factory and had managed to scrape enough money together to move down to a little seaside town, where they started their own little chocolate making shop. Later they expanded into owning a couple of cafes. Naturally those in the family who still worked in the docks and had trouble feeding their large families looked up to the 'the Aunts', as they were known. Their opinion was asked on umpteen different subjects, like the choice of a new baby's name. My grandfather even took the Aunts on his honeymoon.

My father decided to take me to see the Aunts. By this time they had both retired and bought some land on which they built a house with a beautiful garden and employed a maid.

I was the kind of little girl who couldn't really keep still for very long, unless I was buried in a book. On top of that I was always dirty from falling over and tearing my clothes. Meeting these Aunts wasn't a very pleasant experience. With Asperger's its almost impossible to be tactful, as you can't gauge what the other person is thinking, and as our conversations at home tended to be about things like politics, my guess was I must have struck these women as precocious and unruly whilst for my part, I found them formidable, even boring. Dad soon brought me home.

When I was eleven, my father developed an unpleasant ulcer under his tongue, which gave him so much pain when eating that he became progressively weaker and weaker. Finally he had to be hospitalised.

An uncle of ours, who ran our insurance scheme, learnt of our circumstances and offered to have my sister Tara go and stay with them. My father was reluctant to allow this. My grandmother called round to try and coax him into letting Tara go. It was during this visit that somehow or other she let slip that the Aunts had said that they didn't like me. Father took great offense at this and naturally after that wouldn't hear of Tara going to stay with any uncle, and I was certainly never allowed to see the Aunts again.

Before his illness there had been the odd flashpoint of tension between my father and me but after the incident with the Aunts it all got rapidly worse. He went out and bought two thin rattan canes to beat me, which really hurt.

We girls were supposed to help with the household chores while the boys got coal from the cellar and chopped the wood. One day I said to Grant and Clarence, 'Look, I've thought of a real boys' job for you," and indicated the canes and the open fire. I never saw either of the canes again, but usually we were just severely smacked.

I had started attending a little Evangelical chapel and my parents started attending too, although somewhat sporadically. They used to run a 'Ladies' Contact Club' there, which met up every other week, alternating with the 'Men's Contact Club'. My mother went to the ladies' night, but my father would not go to the men's club. He said that if he were to make the effort to go out in the evening, he wanted to see a few pretty girls. At the end of every term they held a mixed party, and my parents went to that. The chapel provided a free babysitting service for those occasions.

One day my father told me that he hated me because I was always trying to come in between him and my mother. This became a self-fulfilling prophecy, because the more he bullied me, the more I turned to my mother for protection. As I grew older it became obvious that I was the one who shared Mum's liking for poetry, and my mother and I would endlessly discuss books. Her favourite was the 'Forsaken Merman' which she knew by heart, followed closely by Jean Ingelow's 'The High Tide On the Coast of Lincolnshire' and Christina's Rossetti's 'Goblin Market'. I think Dad got a bit jealous. He viewed reading as idling and if he saw me reading he would look round for a job for me to do. I used to read a magazine called 'The Girl's Crystal' and he would say, 'Dulcie's peering into the Crystal,' trying to make a joke of me to my younger brothers and sisters. Sometimes he would grab a magazine of mine and throw it into the fire or, more often, tear it up. In fact though he had the whole tenure of the age with him. He once told me that he and a friend were chased out of the public library as children.

My parents had the idea of buying a larger, old war-damaged house to of fix it up for letting out rooms to tenants. This meant that they would sleep downstairs, whilst their children and various lodgers all slept upstairs. One side of Asperger's is severe mood swings. I can remember crying myself to sleep night after night. On two different occasions it was one of our lodgers that came into the bedroom and attended to me. Nothing bad happened to me, but much later it occurred to me that I could have been exposed to considerable danger.

I think I would have been about nine when I started putting my feet onto the struts of the kitchen chairs. My Dad would be onto me in a flash. 'How dare you put your feet on my chairs! This isn't your home, its mine,' he would say. Then came the threats. 'I don't have to have your here. I'll put you in a home, saying you're beyond my care and control'. Then he would make a great show of pretending to ring the police and complain about me. He would pretend that someone on the other end had said, 'Do you know whose children they are?' and he would say, 'Yes of course I do, they're my children.' I realise with hindsight that my father must have had his hand on the bell. That was one of my father's little jokes. Maybe I was supposed to laugh it off? Funny in hindsight perhaps, but very frightening at the time for a young child.

My father also threatened at various times to put me into a home for mentally defectives, saying that he'd been told that they were happy places.

When I was about ten, my mother decided to take an evening job to help make ends meet. She had to work from 5.45pm until 9.45pm every weeknight, and this soon extended to Saturdays as well. With my father working overtime, it fell to me to look after the younger children during the evening. At the time they were all under five and Clarence was then quite a small baby. I had to clear the kitchen table, sweep up, wash up and put four small children to bed, lay the table and get my father's supper ready, and sometimes I had to feed the baby as well. Like so many Asperger people I was very slow at doing things and found this quite a lot of work. When my mother was ill, I had to stay at home to look after the children, and again when my father was ill. I was never thanked ever, and my father was very picky so that no matter how hard I worked it was never good enough.

People I've spoken to about this say, 'Yes, the eldest girl was always expected to help, but you should have had some special privileges.' I never got any privileges, of course.

When I was left in charge of the children, they would always misbehave. Later, when we discussed this, they said they didn't appreciate that I'd been left in charge and mucked around because they could see how nervous I was. They also said they thought it was actually funny to see Dad hitting me.

When I was about ten, my parents bought me a Bible. This was paid for by using the money my grandmother had given my mother for her own birthday. Naturally they gave me a child's Bible with pictures in it. When I entered my late twenties I thought of studying Religious Knowledge at GCE 'A'-level, thinking it would be a walkover with my chapel-going background. As we had to mark various passages, I thought I had outgrown my children's Bible, and logically wanted an adult's version. I asked my parents if I could have a Bible for Christmas. My father duly presented me with another Bible. I opened it but found that Dad had bought me another child's Bible again, with pictures.

When I was about eleven, Dad got a new job working with one of the armament firms in Crayford. Everything Dad's firm made had to be packed at a packing station that was completely separate from the main firm. An overseer had to be selected to make sure that the firm's products were correctly packaged. One day this person was off sick, so they sent my father instead. Weapons destined for Argentina had to be specially greased for going through the tropics, and all the labels had to be typed in Spanish. Debbie, who had to type the labels, was a widow with three small children who lived just opposite this little packing station. Everyone knew how dependent she was on keeping this job, which could be fitted around her family responsibilities. On this occasion Debbie had made a mistake in the typing. Reluctantly my father had to go back and point out her mistake to her. He didn't like doing this, but the shipment had to be correct.

As a chapel-going Christian, father rejected all forms of gambling – he wouldn't even have a pack of cards in the house. So when he was approached to buy a raffle ticket for a lamp in the shape of a ship, Dad refused. Then he was told the proceeds were for Debbie, and for the first and only time in his life Dad bought a raffle ticket.

Later that day Dad heard that the boss wanted to see him. He went in to see him, fearing his wife or children may have suffered some kind of accident. When he got there he was told that he'd won the raffle. But father said that as an Evangelical Christian and a socialist, he felt totally unable to accept the raffle prize. So they raffled the lamp again and got even more money, and my father got a special letter thanking him for doing this.

When I was about twelve, we learnt about 'The Song of Hiawatha' at school, and I was really taken with the lovely rhythms in the verse. Excitedly I told my father about my enthusiasm, to which he said 'Longfellow, he's a bit of a standard one, isn't he? Can't you do better than that?'

When I was about thirteen, my father's employers offered to train him for an architect's position. But this meant that whilst training, he would suffer a massive drop in his pay. Dad asked them if they could possibly give him a bit extra, as he had a large family. They refused, so Dad had to turn the offer down. I have often wondered if this is the point from which he started to become a rather bitter man.

Once, when we were on holiday, I fell out of the top bunk bed. I was badly shaken up by this and had trouble with my feet for a long time afterwards. As usual, Dad thought of it all as a great joke. He often used to dress my grazed knees. As the old dressings came off, he would spit on the open wound saying doctors recommended it.

Once Dad found some saving stamps of mine. These were saved out of pocket money that he himself had given me. He made me go and cash them and hand the money to him, saying he had some bills to pay. This is something I think was really mean, especially as he did not repay me. Once Dad made me cry over something, so I rushed upstairs and shut myself in my bedroom. It was a freezing cold day and I put the electric fire on. Suddenly I noticed it was getting colder and realised my Dad had gone down into the cellar and turned off the electrical master switch.

Years later, when my mother was a widow, I went to see her and asked her why she didn't do anything to stop Dad. She replied that she was always asking him to stop hitting and punching me, but she said she couldn't really do anything because Dad wouldn't take any notice of her.

In 1953, when I was thirteen, Dr Billy Graham launched his first major preaching crusade in this country. My Dad was initially very scathing about all this and said that to the average Englishman, the name 'Billy' suggested a little boy of three riding a tricycle. Later we heard that a member of Billy Graham's Evangelical Team would be visiting one of the churches in our area and some of us, including my grandmother (who didn't often attend church), decided to go along and hear this person instead. Then my father heard that they were running a special train straight to Wembley Stadium and decided that we had to go. I sometimes I think what he really wanted to know was what route the train would take. So my father and I went to hear the famous Billy Graham himself preach. The subsequent experience disappointed my father and he remarked on our journey home that the subordinate that had been sent to preach to us locally was, in his view, a better preacher than the man himself.

Even at that early age I knew I wanted to be a writer, but my Dad always dismissed everything I wrote and gradually, this caused me to loose all confidence in myself. When I left school in July 1955 I was offered a job with the publisher near Bloomsbury. They asked me something that's quite commonplace now: 'What kind of salary are you looking for?' At only fourteen years of age I was taken aback by this and said the first figure I thought of, which they agreed to. Later, when I re-read their advertisement, we found that they had offered the job at about 10s 0d more. This, in those days, was a lot of money. My father was used to working at a factory with a Trade Union negotiated rate where everybody got the same pay, and he wouldn't let me take the job. This would have been my big chance and in fact I've even seen a man's name in the paper where some new author has said, 'He gave me my chance,' and gave the name of the man I would have been working for. I've never been able to forgive my Dad for that, ever.

Both my parents were members of the Labour Party, as is often the case with chapel-goers. Although I found it almost impossible to have much conversation with my father, he did talk to me about politics. In November 1956 when I was sixteen, Britain and France invaded Egypt to try and get the Suez Canal back. My father had some kind of knowledge of Egypt. (I think a relative had served there during the war.) He said that King Farouk was a despot. According to Dad, if the Egyptians had owned the Caledonian Canal, Churchill would have been the first to 'nationalise' it. Father also thought that the claim to have not brought the war to women and children was 'a load of rubbish' and that the amount of publicity given to the troubles in Hungary was 'only a cover for what they are doing in Egypt'. Yet I can't ever remember him using the word 'comrade'. He preferred the older term 'brother/sister' or more usually 'my friends'. He greatly admired and looked up to people like Sidney and Beatrice Webb and George Lansbury. He didn't like our local Conservative MP who, he said, got roaring drunk at her victory party.

At the age of eighteen, I was out of work and had to hand all my unemployment money to my mother. When Dad asked me to pay for something or other, I said I couldn't afford it and he called me a 'meanie' in front of all the family.

Shortly after I'd started work, Dad put me in a bedroom with a particularly dim light. I saved up out of my own money to buy a 100W lamp. One day my sister, Verity, threw one of her mysterious illnesses and Dad came and took my new lamp and put it in her room. When I tried to explain, Dad simply punched me. Finally I decided that the only way to get away from Dad was to leave home, and I started putting all my energies into this end. But I wasn't able to achieve this until several years had gone by.

As a keen cyclist, I wanted a new bicycle. In my mid-teens I had to get my father to sign the hire purchase agreement. Dad came home one day, saying he had seen a bicycle for me. It was a Claude Butler, which was a very good make, and it had an all-welded frame. So he brought it home. It had a very small frame with drop handlebars. At the time I was a big girl of 5'10' and trying to use the drop handlebars gave me a terrific backache. In the end I stopped using them altogether, but I had to go on paying for the bike for another two years. For years Dad would go on and on about the good cycle that he had 'chosen' had been.

Once after I'd left home and was sharing a flat with some girls, Dad suddenly drove up to my flat. I was not expecting him, and when he arrived he found I'd gone out. He was accompanied by my cousin Bernice, who was staying with my parents at the time. Finding me not at my flat, Bernice asked one of the other girls if she could pop in and use the toilet. Later Dad was to go around telling everyone that 'Dulcie lives in a pig-sty as usual' without giving me the chance to explain that Bernice had found the other girls re-decorating the flat at the time.

Presumably Dad was just baffled by my autism, and he was simply trying to punch it out of me. With hindsight I've realised that he probably suffered from a milder form of Asperger's Syndrome himself. He exhibited certain classic characteristics of Asperger's, and other family members would remark at the similarity between us. However, he particularly detested any suggestion that we were alike in any way. One of the things he used to do was always walking ahead of us when we went out together, and seeming to have that lost, abstracted air that is the hallmark of Asperger sufferers. We shared a fascination with the transport system and especially trains. He kept timetables of train routes from all over England and would listen closely on any journey we took for that particular noise that would indicate the route of a train had been changed. He even knew the times of trains leaving Manchester, a city that was some considerable distance from where we lived. I once ventured to ask him if he might consider family counselling (a branch of marriage guidance which counsels children who are unhappy at home). However, after my family's unfortunate experience with the tragic loss of Aunt Jade and then my sister Tara's late diagnosis, they didn't think highly of doctors (particularly any kind of psychiatrist or counsellor) so he refused to see anyone.

As Asperger's Syndrome is completely untreatable they wouldn't have been able to do anything even if we had gone for help. Besides, the only advice we would probably have received would have been not to see each other very often.

Another thing I found particularly irritating about my father was the fact that he was always repeating himself. When I was nursing, he said something about diabetes and turned to me for confirmation. I explained as carefully as I could what the symptoms of diabetes actually were. A fortnight later, when I went home again, he asked me exactly the same question and I gave exactly the same reply. Then when I went again we had the same conversation for a third time, and then again and again. I felt in the end that I just might not have spoken for all the notice he'd taken of anything I'd said. And I could repeat this experience in many other subjects too. This kind of repetition is also typical of

Asperger sufferers are not aware that they are doing it and it is deeply embedded behaviour.

My father was always advising me that I should really serve others and lose myself in some unspecified kind of selfless 'good works'. He stressed that I should be thinking about 'joy in service'. This was also our school motto, which was probably where he'd picked up the phrase. I never really understood what he was talking about. Later he started telling me that there was no beauty in my life. This again, to me, was another silly idea that he'd got hold of and goodness knows what he really meant by it.

If I ever tried to explain anything to him I would barely open my mouth when he would start looking at his watch and saying, 'Look, can you make this a bit snappy, I've got a lot of things to do tonight.' It seemed to me he was always very impatient with me and continually irritated by my presence. When I finally moved out to live with my flat mates, for the first time in my life I was able to let go of that feeling of tremendous fear that I suffered on a daily basis, although after that, I didn't live without my share of problems. I suppose I was a disappointment to my father. Not everyone can cope with an autistic child, especially as they have such a normal appearance. I have friends that have told me that if they had given birth to an autistic child, their partner would have left them.

The Youth Hostel Association movement started organising long distances walks that were really walking races. One such walk was called the Ridgeway Walk and went from Marlborough over the Downs to Streatley-on-Thames. I and my brother Clarence decided to try it out and so booked into a small Bed&Breakfast about some two miles from the starting point. With a great deal of difficulty, I managed to complete this particular walk, and if I include the walk back and to my lodgings I would say I walked about forty four miles that day. I was proud of my achievement. A couple of weeks later, when I was visiting my parents, I mentioned the walk to my father. A little bit later he kept telling me how every member of his family, including me, 'was a bit weak on their pins'. I corrected him, but a few weeks later when I was over there again he was telling someone else that I was 'a bit weak on my pins'. I finished up wondering if my father actually connected to the real world.

If I turned to my mother, she would say, 'Don't be so thin-skinned, you've got to laugh it all off. The trouble with Dad and you is that you both rub each other up the wrong way.'

Towards the end of his life my father became a lonely embittered man. He no longer supported the Labour Party. He said that now politicians 'seem to see it all as just another job'. He wouldn't spend any money on things like the 'Labour Tote' and said that if Sunday is allowed to become just another day, the things that he as a Trade Unionist had fought for, like 'double time' on Sunday, would just disappear. He was horrified at the causes the Labour Party took up, saying they were just 'cheap vote-catchers'. He said the party had been formed because conditions were so bad that a lot of children didn't see their fifth birthday (including some of his great uncles) and that a lot of the founder members were in fact Christians and harked back to the days of Keir Hardie going to Parliament in his cloth cap. He hated having meetings in pubs, he thought of drink as a trick by the bosses to get the working man so doped with drink that he wouldn't think of radical ideas like unions.

Over the years my parents had attended at the little non-conformist chapel more regularly, but Father didn't like any of the new hymns which he said were 'banal, tuneless and difficult to sing and play'. The man who had disdained drink now made his own wine.

However, I have to remember that after the break-up of my first marriage, my father did help me to write letters to various people in connection with my divorce.

I did eventually manage to take over the financial commitments of my former matrimonial home, but was always very short of money, as I was struggling on my own right up until my second marriage.

When I was about 50 my father wrote a letter to my second husband, finally admitting that he had always hated the very sight of me, ever since I'd been a little girl. After that, I had nothing more to do with him although I did go to his funeral, largely for my mother's sake.

Now I've been properly diagnosed I no longer consider that my father blighted my entire life. I think that most families try and scapegoat one particular child who is always blamed for everything that goes wrong in a family, and that person (usually the eldest) was very definitely me. It was a classic situation where I kept going to my father and kept getting rebuffed. Unfortunately my handicap made me vulnerable and I definitely needed help.

My father has been dead for many years now, but it's said your parents are always inside you. Now when they talk about such things as legalising Cannabis I still think I can almost hear my father's voice in the background repeating that 'if it was legal in Jamaica, it was because the bosses wanted you to be so doped-up you wouldn't think of unions'.

Now I try to concentrate on the few good memories I have of Dad from when I was very young, like going to the circus and him showing me round his old school, Monson Road in New Cross. His tenacity made him a good person to have around if any members of our family had a battle that needed to be fought.

CHAPTER SEVEN
Anorexia

It's very difficult to say just exactly when I first started to show signs of developing this condition I was at school during the second half of the Second World War when food was in very short supply and school dinners had just been introduced. Food rationing was then in place, and teachers always seemed to be trying to force feed me with very tough meat, even before I had my back molars. The more they tried to make me, the more I wouldn't – or couldn't – eat. Then of course the same thing started at home. It was just after the war, when there wasn't much money around and food rationing was still very tight.

I didn't like meat and I had endless battles with my father who kept trying to make me eat it. The refrain kept being repeated, 'Well, if you were starving you would eat.' I'm not so sure that this is true, as one of my uncles had been as prisoner of war in Japan and was a vegetarian before he went out there and was still a vegetarian when he came back.

Finally, my mother gave in and applied for a vegetarian ration book for me, so I don't know how old I could have been because rationing was abolished in about 1952. My mother would never do any special vegetarian dishes for me and I was simply served vegetables with cheese. However the battles continued with the school dinners.

In those days people seemed to be quite obsessed with bowel health. It was considered very important to open them every day, without fail. My father (and indeed other people at that time) dosed himself with Andrews Liver Salts every day for that purpose. There were advertisements everywhere for salts: 'Take Enos in the morning to keep you good all day,' and others. Soon he was giving me salts on a daily basis too. Salts look just like white power, but when put with a glass of water they bubble up with an effervescence and, unlike other things, they are pleasant to take.

After a while the salts refused to work for me and thereafter my father started giving me much stronger stuff, like vegetable laxatives and various compounds which were bound to 'do me a lot of good'.

When I moved up to senior school I found, much to my consternation, that they imposed a system of waitress service, which meant that you were no longer given the opportunity to go to the serving counters yourself and select your lunch. On top of this, it would be long time before schools offered any kind of choice and it was widely believed then that a child must eat everything that was put before them. 'You want to see the famished children of Africa', and so on.

This soon meant that I developed a really dangerous eating habit, one minute gorging, the next minute taking laxatives. I also remember solemnly being handed a laxative at a Girl Guides camp when I was eleven. This was the beginning of an eating habit that was eventually to spin out of control, so I was a bit 'bulimic', as they say now.

Even my mother would remark, 'That child's got a healthy appetite.' The fact that I never seemed to put on any weight was put down to a fast rate of metabolism, as I'd always been a fairly active child. But my mother either didn't know about the laxatives and what they were doing to me, or, if she did, she didn't really put two and two together.

When I started my periods, they soon became heavy and painful and I was even advised to take laxatives to deaden the pain, as it was believed then that constipation worsened everything. In fact I was becoming trapped in a vicious circle. My anaemia made my periods painful and heavy, which in turn made me more anaemic. I had to take Codeine to numb the pain. Occasionally, when I was nursing, I would get a sympathetic houseman to write me a prescription for something even stronger. I found that in turn would cause me more constipation, so then I would have to start again and take more laxatives. Doctors weren't particularly sympathetic with this kind of problem. 'Well it'll all be over when you start having babies' was not very good advice for a sixteen-year old. One older nurse I happened to discuss the problem with said she'd been told exactly the same thing but she thought it was all a bit funny. 'No wonder the number of teenage pregnancies has gone up.' Women doctors seemed even less sympathetic than their male counterparts. 'Well, we've all got the same problem.'

After I'd left home, I stopped eating normally and often made do with only a bar of chocolate. This was not uncommon at the time, and a girl I worked with never had a midday meal. She said to me once, 'Oh, you're just not used to it.' Apparently in her family they only ever had one meal a day.

While I was working in Rome as an au pair, the family I stayed with decided to take a walk up the famous Spanish Steps. I was invited along but soon found I couldn't easily manage the incline and, gasping for breath, had to make frequent stops. This surprised me as I'd been mountaineering only a few years before. When I started nursing I had the normal health checks and after blood tests I was found to have a haemoglobin of only 53% (at that time they thought in hundreds, so a normal reading would have been 100%). Naturally I was prescribed iron for a long time, after which I developed brown pigment stains on my legs, which I have to this day. I found out recently that this was a typical result of taking large amounts of iron orally. Finally I was given another blood test and my problems seemed over.

While I was nursing, my appetite seemed to improve, as we were offered a choice of meals that were provided to us free. Our uniforms were also paid for by the state and if you lived in, you had a warm room of your own and a good light to study under. Nurses weren't paid much, but because so much was provided for us – we even had milk put in our rooms in the evening – I found I actually had more spending money than when I had lived at home. Even when I moved out of the nurses' home and into lodgings, as a student nurse I still received free meals in the staff canteen. Most of the local chemists gave discounts to nurses too. A number of us entered nursing at the same time and although a few of them didn't stick to the course, those of us that did became very close, working, studying and living together. I am still in correspondence with some of them. In many ways it was basically a happy, very settled period of my life.

I now had a boyfriend, but he made it clear that he did not want to marry. However, I knew that I could not marry whilst I was training, and I suppose in retrospect I put my head in the sand with him a bit, and thought I could change him. Occasionally he made remarks like, 'I wonder if I will ever meet someone who will really sweep me off my feet,' which I realise with hindsight should have told me that he wasn't really interested in me.

Eventually I left nursing and came to the final break-up with my boyfriend who I had by this time been courting for seven years. I finally realised that I was on a sticky wicket and marriage to him was never going to happen. After nursing I went after a job at the telephone exchange, but for some reason found it very hard-going, so they transferred me to an easier place answering telephone directory enquiries. There was another row with my father at home and I realised that after years away from home, whilst I was nursing, I no longer fitted in, and decided to leave home again.

I changed my lodgings once or twice and tried a Bed&Breakfast place. They always gave me a fried breakfast, and one day I became extremely sick at work and they called in another member of staff who acted as a kind of first aid person. This person got so frightened that she wanted to call a doctor for me. Finally the boss came over. He took one look at the first aid room, which was absolutely covered with my vomit, and gave me the sack.

I got a bad attack of flu (I took my own temperature on one occasion and it was 104), and the flu probably triggered off the anorexia. Recovering from flu pushed my white cells right up, and the iron I'd been taking also gave me mouth ulcers. When I got back to the flat one of the other girls told me that the hospital had been looking for me, apparently they thought I had leukaemia. The weather was very hot around then, which didn't make me feel very happy as I still reacted badly to extremes of hot and cold.

Then the anorexia itself started in earnest. After the flu I just couldn't eat anything. All smells, particularly of food, gave me nausea. I had always been a 'bookish' sort of person and I kept coming across references to 'famine in the world' that had the effect of making me feel guilty about eating. On top of this, I had always been what my mother called 'faddy' about food. By now I was bringing everything back up.

After the flu subsided and my white cell count returned to normal they said they could no longer find anything physically wrong and advised me to see a psychiatrist. Finally I received an appointment and went along, not quite knowing what to expect. After the experience with Aunt Jade, followed by the later experience with my sister Tara, my family wished me not to see one. But the other girls in the flat said that I just needed a bit of 'sorting out'.

I tried to explain the symptoms as best as I could and was put on Stelazine to take three times a day. After that I had to take a depressant to make me sleep and a mild amphetamine in the morning. Basically I was placed on a regime of 'uppers and downers'. Eventually even the doctors could not seem to agree with one another as to what to prescribe to me. I later explained to one of the more sympathetic psychiatrists what his colleagues had been prescribing for me, and he laughed and said the tablets cancelled each other out.

The psychiatrists I saw passed me on to a psychotherapist, or counsellor, as they are often known. I found that those people probably try hard and do a grand job but it remains that they are not medically trained. They usually have a degree in one of the humanities and they've done a course in elementary psychology.

I myself didn't give them a very clear picture. I had no idea that the intense clumsiness that I'd suffered from all my life could possibly be connected to a more serious disorder of neural development. At that time the theories of Doctor Freud still dominated the mental health profession, and in the simple evaluation of whether my problems stemmed from 'nature or nurture', they always came down heavily on the side of 'nurture' and consequently kept urging me to re-live painful memories from my childhood. This caused me months of upset and poor sleep.

For example, when I recounted the sudden death of my infant brother Christopher, instantly they connected this family tragedy with my mental health problems and my possibly having feelings of guilt that I had survived. Grief was a taboo subject then and it did help me a little to talk about that time of my life, but it did not solve my fundamental problems, which were to go undiagnosed for another 20 years. My brother's death had been a very poignant time of our lives, but it did not account for all the things that had gone wrong in my childhood. When Christopher died it wasn't really appreciated that people needed to grieve, and a dead baby wasn't always allowed a proper funeral. Sometimes they even buried about six babies together without a proper headstone.

I recounted all this to my parents and they said it was a 'load of bollocks' that they'd rejected me because their eldest son had died. They had had a proper funeral it seemed, but indeed no headstone, but this was simply because they couldn't afford one. This had meant that they had no place to focus their grief on. In fact, my mother told me that when she'd been carrying Christopher she'd been hoping for a girl anyway. Before he arrived she'd often walked through the cemetery on the way to do her shopping, but after her baby was buried there she couldn't bring herself to go anywhere near the place.

The psychotherapy sessions seemed never-ending and they continued to dig up painful episodes from my childhood. When I mentioned the fiasco of my dancing lessons being abruptly terminated, the counsellor thought this might have been a good thing, because my nerves would never have been strong enough for the stage and sooner or later I would have had to give it all up anyway. Possibly, if I'd had to give it all up much later, the whole thing might have been even more difficult for my parents. As the therapy sessions progressed from one painful childhood event to another, I found my relationship with my parents deteriorated even more, and the gulf between us widened and, sadly, never really healed. Finally the psychotherapy sessions convinced me that my mental difficulties were my parents' 'fault'. I was told that, as the main problem seemed to be with my father, I was advised not to see too much of him because he was never going to change. Apparently hatred of one of your parents is very common with anorexia. They failed to pick this up because the problem parent is usually the mother. So when they asked me leading questions like 'How do you get on with your mother?' this was a point that was often missed.

In fact, I didn't realise that a characteristic of anorexia is to have difficulties with one particular parent. Nobody knows what comes first. Whether you hate your parent because you are anorexic, or whether the fact that you hate your parent has given you the anorexia is not really understood at present. Pat Boone, the singer whose own daughter is anorexic, said that what is known is that the two often go together.

I had booked and paid for another holiday in North Wales, to learn mountaineering. As I'd already paid for it I decided to continue with it. One day it was cold and wet and we went out for a long walk and climb in the mountains, using compasses to find our way. I was paired up with another girl and we both weren't too good with compasses, so we got lost and didn't get back to the youth hostel until nearly 7pm. When we finally got in sight of the hostel, they had already started preparing the evening meal and as I smelt the food cooking my appetite suddenly returned. For the rest of the holiday I ate voraciously and my face soon began to lose its thin, pinched look and my weight returned to normal. I even gained weight.

The 'counselling' that I was undergoing had to be continued. I kept this a secret and told my employers I was going to see the dentist. I hate lying, but I found that people weren't very sympathetic when I tried to explain that I had 'mental problems'. My boss would say, 'A young girl like you, what have you got to be depressed about.' Nobody seemed to pick up the possibility that my problems were organic in nature.

I went through another bout of anorexia and depression when my first marriage broke up, and this time my hair started falling out. Eventually it grew back.

Marya Hornbacher, an American girl who wrote about her anorexia, says in her book that she remembers passing stools that were pure blood. I don't remember any of that, so compared to some people I must have got off lightly. But years later, when I was post-menopausal, I started putting on weight and I asked the family doctor if I should go on a slimming diet. She read 'anorexic' in my case notes and said no, because all my life I would have to be careful in case anything triggered off another anorexic episode.

I mentioned my problems of depression to a nutritionist friend who told me to look very carefully at my diet. The pattern is: you become depressed, don't bother to eat and the depression consequently worsens. She also advised me that my sleeplessness might be the result of too much caffeine and told me to cut down on tea. I now know that low carbohydrates in the diet leads to a slump in mood, particularly in women.

There used to be an agency called the Marriage Guidance Council. It was founded in order to prevent failing marriages from breaking up. Now they have widened their scope to a Family Conciliation Unit to include children who are not happy with their parents, to help stop the thousands of young people who run away from home each year. However, the parents (or parent) who the child doesn't get on with have to go along with them to the counselling sessions.

So, without very much hope, I finally wrote to my Dad asking him if he would come to the Family Conciliation Unit with me. He didn't reply to that letter, or subsequent letters as obviously he had no intention of going. He also told me that the place for psychiatrist's reports was 'in the bin, or preferably in the fire', and that 'a number of learned judges' agreed with him. Sadly this seems to be all too true.

Unfortunately the link between Anorexia Nervosa and Asperger's Syndrome was not made then. I endured years of anguish and disappointment before I was finally diagnosed in my late 50s. No one knew back then that no amount of counselling, psychotherapy or even faith healing was ever going to do me the slightest good. It's now the view of modern psychotherapy not to dig up bad memories and in fact to only refer to them obliquely, because it has been found that re-living past trauma can significantly hinder a patient's progress. However, I do think that 'grief counselling' is an important service that can be given to people when they have suffered the loss of someone significant in their lives.

Dulcie Hall

CHAPTER EIGHT
School and Home

When I first started at nursery school it was September 1944, and the Second World War was still going on. Every morning we had an assembly (then a short religious service) a favourite war-time hymn was 'Through the Night of Doubt and Sorrow'. Obviously the 'Night' was a synonym for the war, and of course 'Onward Christian Soldiers' was another one we often sang. Then came a short prayer followed by the Lord's Prayer. Then we marched out to a lively tune, such as 'Waltzing Matilda'.

If it was a Monday, the teacher had to take the dinner money. This could take quite some time, as we sometimes had 60 children in a class. Someone always seemed to have lost their dinner money or something. Meanwhile we were supposed to be doing sums. At break time, we had cold milk and a glass of orange juice, and something I absolutely hated, a teaspoonful of cod liver oil. I remember trying all sorts of stratagems for getting out of taking it, but none of them ever worked, and I can still remember the horrible greasy taste.

Now, if your child goes to nursery school, they either go in the morning or in the afternoon. We went all day although we might have come out a bit before the big schools. So in the afternoon we had to have a rest and lie on canvas beds for an hour, although I can only actually remember going to sleep once. Sometimes we had to jump out of bed quickly because of an air raid, and I can remember running down the shelter without my shoes on. My mother once asked me what we actually did down in the shelter, and I explained that they had a blackboard in there because even in wartime, lessons had to go on.

When I reached junior school, assemblies were a bit different. The headmaster would often get up to speak to us about something. Usually that meant some kind of moan. Once he twittered on and on about handstands (although I'm not quite sure what he had against them). Then he went on about the evils of eating liquorice wood (then a popular sweet). Another time he announced his disapproval of lemonade powder. At that time you could go into a shop and ask for a pennyworth of lemonade powder and they put a scoop into your hand and you just sucked it off, but the head reckoned lemonade powder had got onto school doors. Then he decided that make up was really our undoing and told us a story about a little girl who was supposed to have come to school with a little bit of lipstick on the end of her fingernail.

When break was over, we all had to stand with our hands against the wall with the first one's hands touching the wall, then the second girl would touch her shoulders, and so on. As we had the infants with us it took a while before we could all lead in and I remember hearing the laundry opposite playing 'Whistle While you Work' then, some kind of pop song.

Back in the classroom came singing, and of course we had to practice the hymns for the morning service. Most of the time, though, we sung secular songs, usually old English golk songs such as 'Madam I Will Give To You The Keys of Canterbury' or 'There was a Little Drummer and He Loved a One-Eyed Cook' or even 'Green Grow the Rushes, O'.

However it was in sewing class that I first started thinking about what I wanted to be when I left school. We had been doing some embroidery with different, brightly coloured wools and I really liked the thought of working with such lovely colours. That was when I first broached the subject of becoming some kind of needlewoman or embroideress when I left school. I even asked my mother if I could possibly be sent to a school that specialised in that sort of thing. However I went off that ambition after some time. Many years later, long after I had left school, I won a first class prize for some embroidery that I'd done, so the desire to be an embroideress can't have left me entirely.

Very poor children received free school dinners, and although we weren't supposed to, everyone knew who they were. The dinners were not cooked on the premises but were brought to the school in large containers on the back of a very big van.

School dinners deserve a chapter of their own. No-one would ever believe how horrible they were. At junior school several older pupils who were called 'monitors' were delegated to lay the tables, which meant putting plastic cloths on all the desks and laying the knives and forks. We were not provided with salt and pepper, but one enterprising boy brought his own and we would mime requests to him for the use of his condiments when the teacher wasn't looking.

My chief memory of school dinners was of stringy potatoes which were always mashed with water, an unidentified cabbage called 'greens' and slices of cold fatty meat which had a very thick fibre. I realise that at the time we had serious food shortages on, but all I remember is the unending battles whilst unhappy teachers tried to make me eat this unappetising food. Sweets or deserts were then known as puddings and usually tasted a bit better, for example milk puddings (occasionally with currants in them), but more usually some kind of very heavy ginger pudding or spotted disk with custard, or perhaps something like prunes. We never had fresh fruit.

At secondary school the whole 'dinner question' was made very much worse because they had a waitress system where some of the girls acted as waitresses. Twelve of us had to sit at very long tables. If you had the misfortune of sitting furthest from the waitresses, it was very difficult to convey your likes or dislikes amidst 10 other hungry pupils.

Shortly after I had moved up to secondary school, the powers that be decided that the Korean War was not going to escalate into a major conflict after all and proceeded to demolish the air raid shelter, building a brand new canteen in its place. Unfortunately the canteen was not big enough to take everyone at once so the children had to eat in sittings. One lot would go in, and when they'd finished clearing up, they would lay up for another meal. On one very cold day, the van bringing the food to our school had skidded on ice at St. Sadie's Hill and was consequently hours late. My sister Tara managed to make it into the first sitting, and while they were waiting ages and ages for their dinner, the teacher supervising that session organised games of 'I Spy'.

Unfortunately one of my other sisters, Verity, was in the second sitting and was stuck out in the freezing cold playground where a gusty wind seemed to have slivers of ice in it. 'Why didn't you come home, Verity?' Mum asked her. 'Well,' she said, 'Another little girl was with me.' 'Next time you come home,' Mum said. 'Bring the other child with you.'

Just after the war there were frantic building works going on, partly because of all the stuff that had been ruined by all the fighting. One day we were talking about making a success in life, and we all talked about how we would show all the people who had stood in our way by telling us that we would not be able to do the things we wanted to do. One girl wanted to 'show' the art teacher by becoming a famous artist, another wanted to 'show' the English teacher by becoming a famous actress. They asked me how I would 'show' the teachers. I've always liked the smell of tar, so I said I would become a steamroller driver and show them by chasing them with my steamroller. At that time steamrollers belched steam and smoke and you could hear them coming. The diesel engines used now never seemed to excite quite the same sense of power and wonder in me.

My sister Dorothy, who is thirteen years younger than me, tells me that they now have introduced the binary laws to junior school, but back then we struggled with feet, inches, pounds, ounces and pints and quarts.

During and just after the Second World War, there was an acute clothing shortage, which was probably the reason why they spent so much time teaching us to knit and sew. First we made a simple dishcloth or flannel by knitting a square, then we were shown how to make a peg bag and finished up by proudly making ourselves an apron. One girl dropped some stitches in what was supposed to be a knitted face cloth. The teacher took it and made a great show of pretending to wash her face with it, while her nose poked through the hole caused by the dropped stitches. 'I don't think that's a very good example of a face cloth,' she said. 'You'd better redo it.' At that time there was no question of us joining the boys for woodwork. Later we went into handicrafts and made things like puppets.

We also had a lesson from the wireless (this of course was before the age of television) and I can still remember Mr Appleby's voice coming over the loudspeaker, saying, 'Hello children, come on, walk tall.' Suddenly he would say, 'Stop fidgeting and find a space and sit down.' Then, 'Imagine you're a soldier.' I heard one teacher remark, 'It's uncanny, but its almost as if he can see them.' At that time we simply called this lesson 'Wireless Lesson' but since then it has acquired the rather suave name of 'Music and Movement'.

I always greatly enjoyed lessons about the Scriptures. It is now called Religious Studies. Stories of Moses in the bull rushes or the Children of Israel's wanderings in the desert seemed very real to me. Reading the Bible again recently, I was struck by how carefully selected the stories really were. At school however, we were taught nothing about the rape of Dinah or just what it was that Potiphar's wife accused Joseph of doing, or the exact nature of the trouble between King David and Bathsheba.

I also greatly enjoyed history lessons. I can remember drawing a picture of the Iceni Queen Boadicea riding her chariot. Looking back I am surprised at how biased history really is. We seemed to be forever learning about Henry VIII's wives. They drummed into us that it had to be 'divorced, beheaded, died, divorced, beheaded, survived' but I can't remember the names of the respective wives of George I, George II or George III. History seems a bit like looking through a long dim corridor that was brightly illuminated in places.

Then came geography, which was again hopelessly outdated and centred round our understanding of Empire and the later Commonwealth. Many years after the communists came to power in China, I remember being taken to the silk factory at Lullingstone Castle and being given a card on better known silk worm diseases and I can remember that silk in its natural state is either white or canary yellow. We did this because silk was one of China's chief exports. Part of Queen Elizabeth's wedding dress was of Chinese silk. I can remember writing that the Chinese people were very afraid of devils and that they had crooked entrances to their homes so that the devils couldn't get in. I wrote that the chief Chinese inventions were silk, tea and ice cream and that they exported a lot of pottery. I didn't know then that in fact the trade embargo had been started with China under the leadership of the United States, and looking back I wonder if any of our teachers knew it either.

English was and always will be my favourite subject. We were always being given the most fantastic stories to write, like 'Describe the Adventures of a Runaway Horse' or 'Getting Out of a Burning Building'. Once in the Burning House story, I wrote that the flames were 'leaping and rearing' and the teacher had crossed it out and put, 'The flames were leaping and dancing – silly.' I realised my mistake but I was most upset. At that time we had to use fluid ink with pen nibs and old-fashioned scratch pens and teachers could hardly read my writing because it was always covered in blots, my clumsiness being an early symptom of my illness.

In fact this clumsiness caused a lot of problems for me at school. I always managed to have accidents with spilt ink. I remember on one occasion I made such a mess with the ink that the teacher said she would have to give me a C for something I'd written. She told me the content is really worth a B, but because there were so many blots on it she would have to give me a C, in case a school inspector saw it and she would get into trouble. I never saw the point of those cumbersome ink pens, if they were meant to encourage greater care with writing, for someone like me, they ended up causing me a lot of wasted time and effort.

Each Christmas we would perform a play and every child dearly hoped for a part in it. One year I played the role of a Red Indian squaw doll who came alive at Christmas. This was only a small part, but it meant an endless amount of trouble for my poor family. My mother was pregnant again and would not be able to come and see the play, but my father looked in briefly and disappeared as soon as my part was over. My mother combed my hair into two long dark plaits and someone lent me a squaw's shawl to wear. We had our small dias made into a large stage and stage hands came in to put up elegant theatrical curtains and glaring footlights. It was all very exciting. The next year they put on a play about a princess who wanted to go to Fairyland and I played the part of the princess's nurse. For this I wore a smart blue dress with a white apron and crossover straps which had been specially bought for me. For both these plays we had to go back to school afterwards and the teacher called our names out one by one and put stage make up on our faces.

Of course I thoroughly enjoyed the part and all the noise and excitement. I've already mentioned some of my ambitions: first a needlewoman, then a steam roller driver, but now I changed my mind once again and decided that what I really wanted to be was an actress. By the time I left school I had changed my mind again and it's just as well I didn't pursue it as I was to be told later that my nerves would never have been strong enough for the stage.

When I was eleven I begged and begged to be allowed to see the first version of 'Julius Caesar' with Marlon Brando and Deborah Kerr. Unfortunately I was in hospital at that time, having my tonsils and adenoids removed. I managed to beg them to let me out on Saturday evening to go see it. I remember closing my eyes tightly during the assassination scene and missed the bit about 'Et Tu Brute'. The film really captured my imagination in a way that few other films or books had done. I became very involved in the mental landscape of 'Julius Caesar' after that and had long conversations with various characters from the story in my mind. I suppose I became a little carried away with it all and actually started dating letters the 'Ides of March'. I also remember asking my mother why Caesar didn't take any notice of the man who told him to beware the Ides of March. 'Well, it would be like warning the Queen about Princess Margaret,' she said. 'Caesar thought of these men as his friends.' One day at school a teacher caught me doing something I shouldn't have and called me over. I replied, 'Wouldst Thou Speak With Me.' She was astounded and remarked, 'I think she's been to see Julius Caesar.'

If you consider this exaggerating: My first husband taught English and specialised in drama. He and some of his friends used to have long conversations about 'Julius Caesar'. 'They shouldn't have needed a figurehead, why drag that fool Brutus into it, why it was him who let Mark Anthony speak,' and so on.

I'm still very interested in acting and I've been in several amateur dramatic clubs, as I have a loud voice that could be heard from the back of the hall. However, after watching Audrey Hepburn in films like 'A Nun's Story' I realised I could never have portrayed the subtleties of emotions like embarrassment the way she does. In fact, my favourite parts are actually comedies, where it doesn't matter if I keep falling over.

I didn't mind not becoming an actress, because by this time I had started praying and was all set for a new career. This time it was the Church. I now wanted to be a very great saint, like a mystic, or a kind of cross between Florence Nightingale and Gladys Aylward.

I had the interest in religion and the enthusiasm, but I doubt with my mental problems I could ever have succeeded as a lady missionary. I wouldn't have been any good at managing people, nor could I really ever have kept a secret. I have always felt burdened by other people's secrets and I would have been hopeless at learning foreign languages. However, one day as I was sitting in chapel, a visiting evangelist seemed to be looking at me when he said how much the Lord needed good writers. I took that to be my 'call' to be a writer. Now I had a new career.

I had a great problem at school with bullying. My mother was later to complain that she was always 'going down that school". The school never did much about it and I have since learnt that Asperger children are targeted by bullies because they can't really relate to other people. Finally my mother said that if I was being bullied, it must be my fault. I tried to make friends with people and although I had friends for a time, it never lasted longer than a few weeks. I was never to have that little girl's great standby, a 'best' friend.

There was another big problem with school: I was always falling over. One week I fell from the climbing rope, a few weeks later from the vaulting horse, but usually I fell over in the playground. Finally, after many such falls, the school suggested to my parents that they have my eyes tested. They did consent to this but all the tests came back normal. I had a cough for a very long time too, and my mother got me checked for TB. The tests were negative, but the specialist suggested to my mother that she get my sinuses checked as I seemed to have some kind of problem in that area.

The secondary school I went to was a fairly new school that had been built in the thirties. The baby boom after the war meant that the school buildings were not actually big enough in the end, so they added a lot of horse huts. These huts were on a separate heating system, but it always seemed that the huts were overheated and the school itself was freezing cold. I always over-reacted to extremes of heat and cold, as a consequence seemed to have a permanent cold.

Unfortunately I was never able to get on with the secondary school headmistress, Miss Hilton. She seemed to lack any kind of sympathy with any of her pupils. Occasionally she used the cane, but her preferred method of punishment was humiliation. One day she told the entire assembled school that one of the girls was pregnant.

Miss Hilton seemed to really have it in for me. Many years after I'd left school I went on a day trip to an expensive seaside resort. Things around there were a bit pricey, so when I saw that a local church were doing a 'coffee morning' run by volunteers, I decided to look in there. I began to chat to one of the women in charge of the refreshments, and I can't remember how the name of Miss Hilton came up, but to my astonishment she told me she'd been to the same school as myself, but not whilst I was there. She said that in her opinion, Miss Hilton had been a perfect demon. My parents had always appeared to blame me for not getting on well with the headmistress, but when I met this lady I felt myself to have been vindicated.

At that time St. Sadie's High Street was full of lots of little fascinating shops. One of the most enthralling was a grocer who had huge aeroplanes on the ceiling that ran across the shop on a curious system of wires. The little aeroplanes went to the cash desk and came back with the change on their black wings. One shop sold pictures and was always worth looking in. Finally there were china and glass shops which were full of beautiful things.

I've already said that you could buy lemonade powder, but you could also get sherbet put straight onto your hand, or even a penny's worth of chocolate powder. In the late forties you could still find the occasional shops where they made sweets on the premises, and there was always a great crowd of children outside watching them, as they were usually made in the window. Some years later, when I was in Soho for some reason, I went into a Chinese shop. They had sweets on the counter and the idea was that you could eat one before buying any, and the atmosphere reminded me very much of an old fashioned English sweet shop.

You can still find the old fashioned sweet shop in some of the older cities and they are worth looking out for, but the real old sweet shop must be a thing of the past. Of course you can still get packets of sweets in newsagents shops, but now that they are full of 'girlie' magazines no self-respecting parent would have sent their child into them alone.

When ice lollies came in (before that, a lollipop was a sweet on a stick) you could buy an ice lolly for a penny. It was real fruit juice, not what you get now, which tastes just like coloured water. Crisps were in larger packets – or maybe there were just more crisps in them – and came with a little bit of salt wrapped in blue waxed paper. Fish and chips were always sold wrapped in old newspapers, and they were always appealing for papers, too. Once in my Labour Party days I saw someone reading the 'Conservative Times'. I asked, 'however did you come to buy that?' and he said that he'd got it wrapped around some fish and chips.

Britain in the late forties and early fifties was relatively crime-free except for small areas. Near us was a most peculiar shop that was owned by an old silver-haired lady probably long past retirement age. Even my father had a bit of respect for her. 'She owns that little business you know,' he would tell people. On one side of the shop she had her library that you had to spend the princely sum of 2 shillings to join, and tuppence per book to take out. She also sold sweets, and lemonade and cigarettes. (This was before the age of pornography.) In the window she had irons and other electrical goods. Her wares might seem a bit of a mix now, but in those days people tended not to specialise so much. One night we heard a terrific crash. At that time the bakers next to us worked all night, so the unarmed baker ran out brandishing his rolling pin just in time to see men on motorbikes disappearing in the direction of St. Sadie's Hill. They had lobbed a brick through the window of the lady's shop, grabbed everything in the window and run off with it.

About a year later there was another raid on the same shop. They must have known it was owned by an old lady who didn't live on the premises. The flat above the shop was inhabited by another old lady who made her living by taking-in knitting. After this second raid the old lady lost all heart and retired, and her shop then became a cut-price grocers. Somehow her little library found its way into my hands and I read most of her books. It seemed as if most of them had been published around the time of the Second World War or just before then. I read them all, but didn't really find anything very new or original in any of them.

Shortly after this, another sweet shop near us was broken into. In addition to selling sweets, comics and newspapers, this shop also sold gifts and fancy stationery. The shopkeeper and his wife lived above the shop and heard the burglary taking place, but as they were elderly they were too frightened to go downstairs and tackle them on their own, so he had the idea to throw his boots across the room and shout out, 'Be quiet, Fred!' Fred was his son who was not there at the time. This ploy made no difference to the burglars who plundered the shop.

Just outside the Evangelical chapel I attended was another little sweet shop called 'The Shed'. It was where we used to while-away the odd half hour waiting for Brownies, Guides or Sunday School to open. (And I fear that a lot of our collection pennies found their way into The Shed.) One day we heard that there had been an attack on The Shed, but the old lady in charge had hit the robber on the head with a ginger beer bottle (in those days stone ginger beer bottles were still in regular use). Naturally everyone at the little chapel heard about it and we all prayed for her and of course we were all very proud of her. One day, long after I'd left St. Sadie's, I was walking past The Shed, having gone back home for something, when I saw a salesman in a car. He asked me if I knew what had happened to the old lady who owned The Shed. I told him about the attack and how she'd fought the would-be burglar off, but he told me that there had been a second attack on her and since then no-one had seen her.

No mention of St. Sadie's would be complete without a mention of 'Smoky Joe', a local tramp who lived in a little den somewhere in St. Sadie's Woods. All the children imitated him and made fun of him. One day some magistrate put Smoky Joe in prison for something or other. But Smokey Joe had discovered that in prison there were nice warm cells and good hot food. So he would cunningly commit a small crime around late September, early October, just so that he got safely 'inside' for the harsh winter months. Of course the winter of 1946/47 was exceptionally cold. After a time the authorities grew wise to it all and one magistrate gave him five years. The shock of being pent up inside during his beloved summer months when he had been used to reigning free and sleeping where he liked was too much for Smokey Joe, and he died in prison.

My mother was always trying to get me out of the house and suggested that I try Woodcraft Folk, but I only went for about 6 months. There were several other things I tried but didn't stick to, but there was one organisation that I really did stick with, and that was the Guides.

For most of the time I spent in the Guides, Zoe Clayton was my patrol leader. The first winter we decided that the Guides would put on a show one evening and parents would be invited along. Everyone was to do some kind of play about a Christmas Carol, and we drew 'Good King Wenceslaus'. I would narrate the story while Zoe would mime the part of the Good King himself and another girl, possibly Eileen Ford, would mime the part of the page and yet another girl would be the poor man. The narrator's part was a good one for me because I had a nice loud voice and I could wear my Guide uniform, so my parents didn't have to buy me an expensive costume.

Unfortunately there was intense rivalry between Eileen Ford, who was to be the page, and Norma Fullerton, who was to be the poor man. Finally Zoe said to Norma, 'Now who do you think should be the page?' After a while Norma said, 'Well, I suppose it should be Eileen,' then added, 'But I'm only speaking out of politeness.' In the end it was Eileen that got the part of the page and Norma was to be the poor man. But Norma got so upset by being relegated to the part of the poor man that on the night of the performance she failed to show up, so we had to get another girl in from another patrol to take her place very quickly.

In addition to these plays, the Guides had hikes and rambles and of course we all went camping. Once a girl from another company was to go in for her Queen's Guide Badge, so we had to simulate an accident and this girl was to prove how she would behave in an emergency. Our guide had to pretend to fall out of a tree and to have sprained her ankle, and this girl was to give the orders on how to treat her. Looking back I honestly think I learnt more about First Aid in the Guides than I did in 10 years of nursing.

In those days we had to learn Morse Code and very difficult it was too. Once we went camping in a place called Beer Head not far from Seaton, and we found out that some scouts were camping on the opposite hillside, and some of the girls signalled with torches using Morse code. I think that that was the only time I've ever seen Morse code being used.

The place I had attended for the short-lived ballet lessons also had a swimming pool in their garden where they taught children to swim. I went there occasionally, but I found open-air swimming too cold. They also had a massive crab apple tree in their garden, which was a bit odd because you don't see many crab apples in private gardens. However, one day I got an even bigger surprise. I had to go round there for something, and I was standing in the hallway when a troupe of monkeys suddenly all marched down the stairs. People wouldn't believe me when I told them, but apparently the place was marked down in the phone book as being a 'monkey hospital'.

There was an old man who had a dog. I once asked about the dog's name. 'I call him 'Dog' because he is one, you see,' answered the man. Another person you saw frequently on the trains around St. Sadie's was an old man who was always reading the Bible. 'What else is there that's worth reading?' he would say.

In St. Sadie's there was a man who had an old banger of a car. Of course most people buy cars to ride around in, but this person had bought their car to take to bits. I would be on a bus and as it went round the corner, the conductor would say, 'Quick! Look and see what he's done to that car now.' One day he'd taken the back wheels off, or another day you'd go past and he'd taken the bonnet off and would be tinkering about in the interior of the engine. One day the conductor said to me, 'A girl in trousers gets on at this stop, always goes upstairs,' and sure enough I soon saw some trousered legs vanishing upstairs. (Girls in trousers were still a rarity in that long vanished time.)

You could still go up the New Road, or the bypass as the older people called it, and I can remember taking my younger brothers and sisters – I was still at junior school, so I couldn't even have been eleven – and staying up there all the morning picking blackberries. Because of the food shortages which still existed right up until the early fifties and beyond, these blackberries were welcomed for their food content and my mother was especially keen to feed our latest baby on the blackberry juice.

At secondary school we repeated a lot of what we had already done at junior school, but one thing we did have was cookery lessons. As I'd had to help in the house a lot, learning it all afresh seemed a bit odd to me. Also we had to learn how to bath a baby, which also seemed a bit funny to me, as I'd been bathing babies nearly all my life.

In many ways my schooldays were a complete and utter failure. I never learnt to climb a rope because no one had ever shown me how to lever the rope using my knees. I never learnt to swim, although a lot of time was spent teaching me. Arithmetic was taught badly and we never did any algebra, geometry, physics or chemistry and were given no homework. Mathematics teaches you to think logically, and that's something I never learned.

If my school days hadn't been blighted by my mental illness I might have got something out of it all. However, I did have some bright moments and still have a few happy memories of that far off time.

CHAPTER NINE
New Dress

Like most autistic and Asperger people I know very little about clothes or what suits me, so buying clothes has always been very difficult for me.

As a child, with both my parents being Labour supporters, we used our local Co-Op. There, they used the 'divvy' system, as we got our milk and groceries from the Co-Op. This usually came to something and was a very great help to my mother.

Buying clothes from the Co-Op always entailed a trip to either Lewisham or Woolwich, although sometimes we combined the two and got a bus from Lewisham across Blackheath to Woolwich. Naturally this was always a great outing and sometimes resulted in a visit to a cafe, but not often, because my parents thought that it was pointless to go in a cafe when you could cook everything you wanted at home. Nevertheless it was exciting and sometimes, if it was near Christmas, it might entail a visit to Santa Claus as well, as all the big department stores had them.

As I grew older, my enjoyment of shopping trips gradually gave way to wrangling, as my perception of what suited me began to differ greatly from that of my mother's. From the age of about sixteen all shopping trips began to end in tears.

When I left school, I started work in a London department store and finally had some money of my own. Now I could buy what I liked. It was August 1955 and I was to receive £3.30d. out of which I had to give £1.00 to my mother for my keep. A further 10/- was for train fares and 10/- kept back for lunches. This left me with a whole £1.00 to spend. However, I also had to save money for holidays and there were Christmas presents to buy for my younger brothers and sisters, all of whom would be expecting something 'good' now that I was working.

For the first time I could buy my own clothes, but my mother continued to influence my choices. 'I've seen a pinafore dress in Finlays,' (a shop in St. Sadie's High Street) my mother told me, 'It's only 19s lld.' I felt obliged to buy it, but how I hated it. With my thick black hair, grey was not a colour that suited me, and the shape and style of the dress reminded me of the old-style school gym slips that I had only recently outgrown.

As autumn crept in and the weather grew colder, I had to wear a grey jumper over it. This one had been bought because it was cheap and was supposed to have 'batwing' sleeves. I thought it looked shapeless and disguised my best feature, my figure. I kept looking at things in shops, but as I could only manage about 5/- per week towards clothes, there didn't seem to be much within my price range. I did manage to buy a yellow cotton dress that I picked for myself from a shop in St. Sadie's, but the first time I washed it the hem went in all different lengths and I realised that I had made a very bad buy.

The stockroom of the shop I worked in became freezing cold during the winter of 1955/56, and when a newcomer was offered more money than me I decided to look round for another job.

For my second job I went to the stockroom at the John Lewis Partnership in Oxford Street, where my pay there was £3.l0s. In theory this gave me more money to spend on clothes, but at the same time the cycling club that I had joined put pressure on me to buy a better bicycle, so I had to get one on hire purchase, and that didn't give me much money left over.

I had other problems. I didn't really realise this at the time, but by putting me into a shop my parents had chosen a line of business that isn't really very well paid. Of course there were a lot of people in my position with regard to money, but they all seemed to have a route to improved circumstances that was not open to me. Lorna for instance earned the same money as me, but her parents would only take 10/6 a week from her. Maria, an Italian girl, earned even less than me, but her parents allowed her to work in a cafe in the evening whereas my mother wouldn't hear of it. Carol's mother helped her cut out and make a lot of her own clothes (a very great saving) and Thelma's mother cut her hair which also meant that Thelma had more money than me. Joyce's mother let her cycle into London every day, but my mother wouldn't let me, as she said I would arrive there all hot and sweaty, and department stores wanted their girls looking nice. Actually I was still trying to get employment in a shop that offered boarding facilities, as a number of them did then.

I was still determined to try and save enough money to leave home. However my efforts were thwarted, because as soon as I managed to save some, my father would find out about it – he often went through my savings books – and demand I give it to him because he said he had some bills to pay. 'You don't need this money,' he would say. 'Look, you won't go on holiday till the summer and Christmas is a long time away.' I was supposed to get the money back as it was supposed to be 'only a loan' but as I remember it, I was only occasionally paid. I've since realised that my Dad just couldn't handle money.

There were other problems. I wasn't allowed to wear make up. My father said lipstick came off on the cup and wasn't clean. When my sister Tara came home with some eye make up on, he went into one of his frenzies and said that if any women came into his house with 'duck egg green on her eyes' he would take a stick to their backside. Apparently my Dad was gripped in a bit of a time warp because he must have been remembering when at one time they used to put things like arsenic in make up. These practices would have emerged in the twenties when he would have been a young man. He also said that make up was overpriced and that it could possibly deceive men about your real age. (Although I was in my second job, I was still only 15, and below the age of consent.)

My Mum and I tried hard to make my Dad see that for a young woman working in the West End, make up was looked seen as a 'finish', particularly for a shop that sold make up.

Another cause for argument was that my Dad wouldn't let me wear a bra. He said that they were an American idea they had invented to get your money. I said this to someone at work once and she said, 'Does your mother wear a bra?' I didn't know and wouldn't have dared ask her. Apart from all that, I didn't get much opportunity to speak to my mother privately, as she still worked every evening and most of Saturday.

Of course I did get a chance to buy things that had been reduced while working in the stockroom of a department store, and so I was able to buy a red and white pinstriped skirt that a customer had returned for some reason. I was really pleased that this proved to be a very good buy. But I was still desperately short of clothes. Most of the clothes that places like John Lewis and other Oxford Street shops sold were far too expensive for me.

Then one day just before Easter in 1957, a line of 'special offer' dresses came into the stockroom. One of them immediately caught my eye. It had a white nylon background with green, mauve and pink flowers picked out on it. It had a crossover top with a narrow bodice and a three-tiered skirt. It was a dress that I just had to have.

Normally John Lewis staff received a reduction on clothes that they bought for themselves, but as this was a special line there would be no staff reduction. I did secretly manage to try it on and hurriedly put a reserve notice on it. Every single day after that I went to look at it, and the more I looked, the more I wanted it. The price was just 29/6p. After long arguments and calculations with my mother it was agreed that perhaps with savings in other directions, I could just manage it.

Then one day the girl in charge of ticketing this particular line of dresses came over to me and asked if I was still interested in that dress. I said, 'Yes, of course,' and she said, 'They are going over to the main shop now.' I knew putting a reserve notice on it would not work because it was a special line.

The John Lewis store I was working in had been bombed during the war, and rebuilding work was going on at the time. The dress would be transported to the East House (so named because it was part of the old building) while I worked in the West House. It was then about 10.00am. The first opportunity I could get to visit the shop floor would be during my lunch hour at 12.30pm. Of course I would need to get the necessary money out of my Post Office account in time. All morning I was on tenterhooks, supposing someone were to go into the East House and were to see 'my' dress and buy it. Finally it was lunch time and I raced out, drew out the necessary cash and rushed over to East House.

As I walked into East House I was trembling with anticipation, as the dress had been in the shop for two whole hours now. Just supposing it had been sold? Incredibly my dress was still there, hanging on the rail. 'You know you won't get a reduction,' the girl told me, but I couldn't wait and bought it there and then without even a second try-on. I couldn't believe it, I finally had 'my' dress in my hands. It remained my favourite dress for many years to come.

My parents had become staunch chapel-going Christians and, as such, of course were also supporters of the Labour Party. Around this time, Hugh Gaitskell became leader of the Labour Party and, ever mindful of the 1959 general elections looming, began a tour of the marginal constituencies of which St. Sadie's was one. As I was Secretary of the Committee of the Young Socialists, I was chosen to present a bouquet to Hugh Gaitskell's wife, Dora. The press were following Gaitskell around and there was a chance that a picture of me might even appear in the paper.

Naturally I decided to wear my favourite dress for this occasion. At the time it seemed a great success; we all stopped and chatted with Mr Gaitskell and his wife seemed a very nice lady.

Unfortunately things didn't go as planned. The picture in the paper, when it appeared, didn't show me at all and, worse still, the Labour Party lost the 1959 election, and a few years later Hugh Gaitskell died and was never to become Britain's Labour Prime Minister after all. By the time Gaitskell's successor, Harold Wilson came along, all Labour Partly advertising was done on TV and Wilson never made the personal tour of the constituencies that Gaitskell had done, but by that time I had left home anyway.

Looking back Gaitskell seems more of an idealist, the last perhaps, of the old socialist school. Or does it seem like that with the advantage of hindsight?

I last wore 'my' dress on a visit to St. Paul's with some Argentinean visitors some time in the late 1970s, well before the Falklands War.

The dress remained my favourite for many years and it's now almost fifty years since I bought it. I regard it as my first major purchase made of my own volition, therefore marking the beginning of my adulthood.

I looked at the nylon dress again recently but now with middle-age spread sadly I am no longer able to fit into it. I can truly remember the day I bought it as if it were yesterday. I suppose it must have been a rite of passage.

CHAPTER TEN
MOTHER

There is no doubt at all that my mother, Edith, had a profound influence on my life. In many ways she tried to get me to do the things that she wanted to do herself, yet was unable to, as she'd had a traumatic childhood.

Mother was a tall woman, on the plump side, but not quite stout. She had hazel eyes and dark hair. When she was a young woman she wore her hair in a centre parting, which often caused people to wonder if she was a continental.

When Edith returned home to live, her sister Ruby was hoping to earn her life-saving badge and taught Mother to swim on her back. This enabled Ruby to practice the life-saving technique on her. Mum is the only person I know of who was able to float before she could swim. She and Ruby would go to the baths in the early morning. Often they were the only people there.

Mother was a keen cyclist; she went everywhere with her sisters Ruby and Beryl. Mother once claimed that she, Ruby and Beryl were amongst the first women to wear shorts. Mother liked to tell us about how she and her sisters were waiting for the dawn to come up so that they could cycle to Brighton. 2.00am came and they got fed up with waiting, so they decided to go. Mother remembered seeing the dawn rise over Red Hill that day. When they finally reached Brighton, they went to sleep on the beach. Later they woke up and came home, ensuring my mother was back in time to teach in Sunday school in the afternoon. Mother and her sisters also cycled down to the Isle of Wight, passing the 'Devil's Punchbowl'. Mother liked rambling too, and enjoyed going out with the Rangers (she was never a guide) and cooking their own meals over a camp fire. In addition to that, she joined a rowing club. Mother also became quite a keen photographer, saving up for the latest 'Brownie' camera with the latest gadgets. To cut costs they did their own developing and printing. One photo that she was particularly proud of showed their dog 'Nyp' jumping, caught with all four of his legs off the ground.

My parents bought me a fairy cycle when I was about four. I learnt to ride it and got another when I was about nine or ten. I finally saved up to buy a second hand one when I was about 13, at £4, which was a lot of money in those days.

When I was about six, Mother saw a set of Arthur Mee's encyclopaedias in a second hand bookshop. As they had a volume missing they were being sold cheaply, so she grabbed them. These books introduced me to a lot of new things, like making my own tent and creating an entire 'Eskimo village' out of cotton wool and upturned eggshells. I made the icy lake from glass and a kayak using an old matchbox. In those days we improvised a lot of toys and made our own train sets with matchboxes for the carriages, and cotton reels for the wheels. The story section of the encyclopaedia was very good, too. In addition to this, there was a good section on history and poetry, which doesn't really date. I spent ages going through these volumes.

When I was about seven, Mother left me in charge of my younger siblings whilst she went back to Bressington to change her ration books. She was heavily pregnant at the time and it would have been awkward for her to get small children on and off buses. While she was out, one of the children crawled round and turned the gas tap on. It was a nice day, so I took the children into the garden. Afterwards we found out that Mother could have changed her ration books in St. Sadie's, but no one had told her.

Mother also taught me to knit and sew. I remember watching her make a complete baby basket from an old tomato basket, together with little nightdresses for the coming baby. This was quite impressive, given that she didn't really like sewing.

After she got over her initial shock, Mother was always a tower of strength in any crisis. She would rub camphorated oil on my chest if I had a cold and give me onion porridge. For coughs, she would mix real butter with black treacle and very hot water to sip whilst hot. Milky, well sugared tea, and a hearty meal would be bound to lift depression. She grew her own mint and parsley and made her own sauces.

Looking back, my mother always seemed to be cooking. During the war she preserved bottles of fruit and homemade jam and on one occasion she made her own lemon curd. Later on in the new house she made gingerbreads, jam tarts, and iced her own cakes. She made pastry, including flaky pastry, never using a cake mix, which she frowned on as 'tricks to get your money'. She would never buy grated cheese or minced meat, preferring to grate or mince her own. She used to say that she just knew that they grated the cheese and minced the meat that they couldn't sell. She wasn't that keen on sausages either for a similar reason and didn't really like fish paste or pâté.

For breakfast on Sundays we had eggs and bacon, fried tomatoes and fried bread. My mother would often say, 'Cor, fit for a Kingie' as she sat down to eat. After breakfast, if our plates were greasy, we were expected to take a piece of bread and wipe our plates with it, eat it and continue to eat our toast and marmalade off the same plate, continental fashion.

On Sunday dinner we had either roast beef with Yorkshire pudding or a leg of lamb. For sweets we had apple pie and custard, or, in later years possibly, a choice of that, or apricot flan.

Whilst we were at afternoon Sunday school Mum would get our Sunday tea ready. There would be peaches with Libby's milk and homemade fairy, or negress cakes, called 'drop-deads' rather jokingly by my father. Often we had visitors, although my parents had few friends, as they both came from large families and could always make up for it with relatives.

In addition to the above, Mother was also a very keen gardener. This led to a bit of tension with my Dad, because he came from New Cross and had grown up knowing nothing but streets, streets and yet more streets and thought it was nice to have flowers. Mother, having grown up in the country, looked on the garden as the place to grow food. During the 'Dig for Victory' campaign he went along with her to a certain extent, but afterwards he said he wanted flowers and started digging up things that my mother had planted.

When we moved to St. Sadie's the people moving in to our old house had told us that they would be parking their car at the side of the house. That was where Mother had a favourite pink peony, so she dug it up and brought it with her. I'm afraid the pink peony never did very well at the new house and eventually died, but we did inherit a beautiful blood red peony which we split into two.

Eventually Mother managed to persuade Father to shorten the lawn and grow some fruit trees. Father did and planted some cherry trees, but then we found that the neighbours' children took them. This led Dad to plant some ornamental poison cherries. After all, he reasoned, the neighbours' children might eat sweet cherries, but they'd be bound to leave these cherries alone.

Unfortunately the neighbours' children didn't realise that the cherries weren't really suitable for eating and mother had her work cut out for her to try and stop the neighbours children getting poisoned. Mother pressed on, dreading herself being blamed by crowds and crowds of angry parents. Every Sunday morning Dad swept up the dead leaves and lit a fire to burn them. Much to Mother's annoyance he always lit a fire in a different part of the lawn. Talking to him did nothing; he would say he was sorry, but did exactly the same thing again the following Sunday.

Later on, there was to be another problem. In order to supplement their limited income, my parents started taking in lodgers. We had one lot of tenants who caused us endless trouble, and eventually my parents had the locks on all the doors changed, put all their belongings in the front garden and told them they had to go. They called in the police, but in the end they did in fact go.

When my father unfortunately became ill, I remember it was a very difficult time for Mother, as she was not only very worried about Father, but she also had far less money on which to manage. Everything seemed to go wrong. Libraries were pressing for the return of library books that we couldn't find, and all sorts of people were pressing us with their bills. Mother wrote long letters to all our creditors. The gas and electric people were threatening to cut us off, and we were being pressed to pay rates as well. Then we heard the council was going to send the bailiffs round to seize our furniture for unpaid rates. Shortly before that day arrived, Mother found an old dresser that she didn't particularly like and decided that if they were going to take something it had better be that.

'I'm sure bailiffs are very lazy people,' Mother said. 'Lets move everything out to the front hall so that they will see it.' With much pulling and tugging and dropping parts of it onto our toes, we finally managed to get the old dresser out to the front hall. 'There you are, they can take these things.' Mother found some old white board and wrote 'Very Valuable' on it in big letters. 'I'm sure that when they see that, they will never get any further than the front hall.' 'Are you sure that that old thing really is valuable?' someone asked her. 'If they hold onto it long enough it'll be an antique,' Mother assured us. 'Perhaps they will think we are trying to tell them something,' Grant commented, looking round. The dresser in the hall made it difficult for anyone to get past. 'Well, we are, aren't we?' someone else said.
The day the bailiffs were due finally arrived and we all waited with bated breath to see what would happen. Then the postman delivered a letter that said the following:

'Dear Mrs Hall,
We have read your letter and understand your position. Under the circumstances we would not dream of sending in the bailiffs. We understand that we will be paid as soon as you are able.
Yours faithfully,'

Of course this meant that we were soon hard at work putting the dresser back. The trouble was that Dad couldn't budget and indeed was always taking time off work with some mysterious illness. When in hospital he would often take his own discharge, then he'd try and do a lot of overtime to make up the deficit and before we knew where we were, he would be ill all over again. Many times he was referred to a psychiatrist, but always refused to go. If my own experience is anything to go by, I rather doubt they would have given him any real help if he had.

Apparently Mum asked Dad if she could take over managing the family money, because she had a Jewish background and a head for figures. My father wouldn't hear of it. 'You always want to wear the trousers!' However, I promised Mother that one day, when I could afford it, I would take her to the theatre and buy her a gown.

Mother always put a lot of thought into buying presents, and although she didn't have much money, everything she gave us always turned out to be something we really wanted.

One day, I came home from school to find Mother struggling to put up another bed. I asked her what the problem was and she said that my Aunt Garnet had been admitted to a mental hospital as a voluntary patient, and that uncle Crispin was sending my cousins Bernice, Hope and Swithin over in a taxi. They were expected to arrive within the hour. My cousins duly arrived, but as a child I didn't notice how much my mother was worrying about my aunt, only just how jolly it was to have all these cousins staying with us. One night we had a midnight feast. I can't remember what we ate, but I can remember bursting balloons. When we told Mother about it the next day she said, 'Well, its a good job I didn't hear you, otherwise I would have been in there handing out the smacks.' Unfortunately my aunt's breakdown was to prove the first of many and we had my cousins on several visits. Later, as they grew older, they came over on their own.

I must have inherited my love of literature from my mother. As a tiny child I can remember sitting on her lap and being read to aloud by her. A. A. Milne, 'Peter Pan', 'Alice In Wonderland', 'Just William', 'The Water Babies', 'Little Women' and many more. As I grew older and read for myself, she tried to introduce me to different authors such as Edgar Rice Burroughs, Angela Brazil, Talbot Baines Read, Edith Nesbit and indeed many more. Later on she joined the World Book Club and introduced me to Rumer Godden's 'Black Narcissus' and Richard Llewellyn's 'How Green Was My Valley' among others. Sometimes she saw a film, then went and read the book. In this way she found 'Gone With the Wind'. Later she nudged me in the direction of Charles Dickens and George Eliot. As I grew older, the traffic became two-way and I introduced her to several new authors. We endlessly devoured, discussed and dissected books, plays and poetry.

It all happened so slowly that I can't quite remember when it started or how it happened, but Mum gradually began to shut me out of her life. My father had a serious illness when I was 11 years old, and perhaps it started then. When I was 15, we went on a family holiday to a camping coach in Blue Anchor Bay. It was entirely self-catering and when we got there it was all paraffin cooking and Mum, by this time pregnant again with her last child, had a lot of morning sickness (as I was later told) and thought I hadn't helped her much. The way I remember it was that they were always leaving me in charge of the children whilst they went out somewhere. But she became increasingly snappy with me and did little things to make me feel out of it. One day she called all the children together, except me, and told them that there was to be a new baby brother or sister. Then, when her uncle died and left her some money, she made a point of telling everyone in the family bar me (I found out later about this), and so on. She started uttering dark threats about how Tara would take my place in the family. As I'd never been conscious of having a 'place' of any kind in the family, this didn't really make much sense to me.

I still tried to talk to my mother about books, but steadily and imperceptibly she pushed me away. When I was about 16 or 17 they released the film 'War and Peace'. After seeing the film I rushed and got the book out of the library, and when I'd read it, I tried to get my Mum to read it. She wouldn't and kept making disparaging remarks, saying that she and Dad had lived through War and Peace and didn't want a reminder of it. Nothing I could say would shift her position on this.

Another time she told me that I was 'always miserable'. Later I realised that perhaps part of the reason for my continued low spirits was the fact that I wasn't eating properly, and perhaps teenage hormones came into it too. I started having bad nightmares, but when I tried to tell Mum about it she remarked rather tartly that if I had to work as hard as she did, I would fall asleep as soon as my head hit the pillow. Whilst I'd been at junior school some years before, I had gone through a bad attack of bullying. My mother started to keep bringing this up and now said it must have been all my fault. I was deeply estranged from my father, who was continually hitting me (usually over something very trivial) and generally putting me down and making fun of me. Of course I've since found out that sleeping problems and being targeted by bullies are part of autism.

Now that my mother seemed to have turned against me as well, I started planning in earnest to leave home. I made all sorts of plans which didn't work and finally only managed to leave home when I was about 19. I was still expected to send money home; my parents said that if I didn't, they would let my room out. Even much later, I still sent occasional money to my mother, which I didn't mention so that if my father saw the letter he wouldn't know. Then she would reply, 'I've received your letter and enclosures...' I suppose that even at that late stage, I loved mother very much and still desperately wanted her to love me.

Once, after I'd left home, she wanted to borrow a large sum of money from me and promised to pay me back out of my sister Verity's college grant. Another time she asked me for some money, promising to pay it back out of my grandmother's estate, but my grandmother was still very much alive at the time.

After I'd left home I didn't see too much of my parents for a long time. They never seemed all that anxious to see me, and I only really got to talk to my mother again many years later, after she had become a widow. I asked her then why she had never come to my defence when Dad kept hitting me, and she said, 'I was always telling him to leave you alone, but I couldn't do anything because he wouldn't take any notice of me.' I suppose then I didn't really grasp the complete helplessness of women in marriage.

Mother now joined a Creative Writing class and tried to get some of her own work published. She told me that an article of hers on collecting First Day Covers had been printed in 'The Lady', but she had a dry sense of humour which isn't really appreciated now. Once, many years before as a waitress at Lyons 'Corner House', she had written a poem about her life as a 'Nippie'. Just one verse sticks in my mind:

'Waitress, here my soup is cold' 'Waitress, where's my tea?'
'I ordered water first' I'm told 'Oh, how they shout at me'

She tried to get it published in the Lyons in-house magazine but they thought it implied criticism of Lyons, so they wouldn't take it. I do wish she had pushed that side of her life much more.

Mother once told me that when she was at school, her geography mistress always told her to travel if she ever got the opportunity. So when she was young, Mum looked up what you needed to emigrate to Australia or New Zealand. The only way to go seemed to be doing housework, and as Mother knew she would hate that, she didn't apply. She was brought up to look on things like foreign travel as we would a trip to the moon: reserved only for the rich.

Some years later Mum had the opportunity to go to Bavaria with some women from her place of work, and I believe she thoroughly enjoyed it. Then my parents saw a trip to Romania advertised and it was so low in price that it was as cheap to go there as it was to stay at home, so they went.

Both she and Dad were later to say that you couldn't be in the country for five minutes before realising that the people there all hated communism and would really have liked to side with the West. Whilst dining in a restaurant there they actually saw President Ceausescu, seated a few tables away, and watched as a little girl got up and presented him with a little posy of flowers. Shortly after they returned to England, communism collapsed.

After she became a widow, Mother decided on one last holiday with some people from her church. She had long wanted to visit the Holy Land, and finally some churches in her area organised a large group of people to go there. Mother was amongst them. She came home absolutely full of it. They had stood by the pool at Bethesda and whilst they had stood there the tour guide had read from the Gospel Story, and of course there were many other stories. Then a full photograph had been taken of Mother and the others in the group, and Jerusalem can clearly be seen in the background. Mother was later to say that this was the best holiday she had ever had. She still kept up with the other group members for a very long time afterwards.

After she had been widowed for some time, Mother had a birthday coming up and I wondered what to give her. However, my church had organised a day in Bruges, Belgium, and I thought of offering to take Mum on the understanding that we would pay for her, but she was to provide her own spending money. She spent the night before at our house, and early in the morning we caught the coach, which raced to Dover, getting there at about 9am. Then we went to Calais and the coach reached Bruges at about lpm. We got a really funny little horse drawn bus up to the centre of Bruges, and after some lunch we had a trip round the canals. Mum always enjoyed everything to do with boats. After that we had a sumptuous continental tea with pastries and just enough time to buy some lace before getting the coach back to Calais. Mum told me that she thoroughly enjoyed it and she told other people that, too.

In many ways I've done the things Mother wanted to do but wasn't able to. When I saw a rainbow in Venice, I wished my mother could see it as well; when the bus I was on in Athens came round the corner and I saw the Acropolis for the first time, I thought how much I wanted Mother to share this moment with me. When I saw the Blue Mosque in Istanbul, I thought Mother should see this, and the same with the view of the Eiger in Switzerland. I know how much she would have enjoyed it all.

In many ways I would have liked to have been more like my mother, who was the sort of person people went to when something was wrong, like my uncle Stanley when he came back from the Far East, and my cousins when their mother had a nervous breakdown. But I never could be like her because of my mental condition.

As she grew older, Mum's memory started letting her down and she told me that it gave her a lot of distress that she could remember things very clearly that happened when she was a child, but struggled to remember what day her grandson was coming to visit.

Then, my brother Grant started getting calls from Mum's neighbours, saying that they thought they could smell gas. It seemed that Mum's sense of smell had gone. Then, she lost the ability to tell the difference between night and day and was found wandering around with her shopping trolley in the middle of the night until she was eventually stopped by the police. One day she was on the doorstep and said, 'I keep knocking, I can't think why they won't come and let me in,' and we looked and saw it was her own house that she had been knocking at. Once again both my sister Verity and myself asked if she would come to live with either of us. She refused, so clearly the time had come to put her in a home.

My sister Dorothy had taken Mother on holiday with them and they'd stayed in a hotel, so my sister and brother told Mum that they were taking her to a big house, a bit like a hotel, and that the people there would take care of her. So early in January 2001, they took her to a residential home for the elderly. She wasn't very happy there and a great open sore developed on her leg from some kind of unexplained wound. She had tried to come home in the middle of the night and the staff of the home went outside to fetch her back. It looked as if she'd been dragged along the ground or something, but she wasn't able to tell us about it. So she was moved to another home and then into a third, where she finally seemed to be much happier. It's sad today to see her lose her independence, but we go in and see her whenever we can. We have taken her out by car to some of the places she used to cycle to when she was a young woman. When I go to see her I often take her for a walk round the park, as I know she loves the open air and used to do something to her garden every day.

Sadly, Mother no longer recognises any of her children, but she does know that she's in a home. Sometimes I think of the poem she liked so much, 'The Forsaken Merman', about the girl who, once back in the world, could no longer remember her own family, and I think how strange that it should have come about in her own life.

When I was a little girl, my Dad bullied me, but Mother was never able to mount much of a defence. Now I can see that this was because she lacked confidence. So maybe it would be interesting to look at Mother's childhood and see the forces that shaped her and made her what she was.

CHAPTER ELEVEN
Those who went before

My mother, Edith, was born in 1911. She was the third born into a family of 15 children. In September 1914 at the age of three she started proper school, as in those days they tried to teach quite small children reading and other things. She was very unhappy and kept crying, so the teacher finally said, 'Right, I'll give you something to cry about,' and laid Edith across her lap, lifted her clothing and hit her hard, thus making her cry even harder.

Then Edith came home from school with a sore throat. A doctor diagnosed croup and he told my grandparents to get a steam kettle. Granddad went all over London looking for one (not many chemists were opened on a Sunday then) but when he finally got home with it, he found that in fact Edith had diphtheria.

They rushed her to hospital but found that hospital after hospital was filled to bursting point with the troops. The Royal Free Hospital annex on Rosslyn Hill, Hampstead, said that they would send out an ambulance in the morning. 'If you wait until morning I must just as well sit down and write this child's death certificate,' the doctor said.

It was close to midnight when an ambulance driver carried Edith into hospital, gasping for breath, her terrified parents following, already worried about the disease spreading to the rest of the family. She was taken straight into the operating theatre and given a tracheostomy there and then, with no time for an anaesthetic. Soon she was breathing normally, but it had been a very close call with death.

Edith's recovery was complicated by the fact that she was malnourished and suffered from rickets. The doctor suggested that she should have a long convalescence in the countryside. 'We are a working class family,' Granddad said. 'We can't afford it.' 'Well,' the doctor considered, 'Maybe she could stay with relatives in the country and eat proper food, as she's not out of the woods yet.' So my grandmother asked her parents if my mother could stay with them. In early December Edith, frightened and tearful, was taken to the station clutching her beloved doll.

Leaving the train, they walked down a lane which soon became a narrow, stony track, slightly wider than a footpath. As it wound through the fields Edith saw lights glimmering through the trees that seemed to take the form of a human face. Then they arrived at the farm.

Walter and Eleanor came to the door to meet her and took her to the Boot room. Outside the house boots were worn, but indoors it was slippers, it was a rule. 'No slippers? Well, perhaps a pair of Mary's will fit you.' It was an old house that had a Tudor Rose and '1578' inscribed over the door. The kitchen had a well, and it was in the form of a huge water wheel that one had to stand in and walk to draw the water up. 'We always fill a kettle with water every night,' Eleanor explained. 'The well has a nasty habit of icing up and we might need hot water to unfreeze it.' They lit the oil lamp and hung it from a hook in the ceiling, making pools of light with deep shadows at the corners of the room. In the centre of the kitchen was a large oak table and as they had guests, Walter turned a little handle that extended the table, and extra panels were placed in the middle. An open log fire kept the room warm and there was a side oven and a bread oven. Over the hearth hung a notice:

'God is the Head of this House
The Unseen Guest at every meal,
The Silent Listener to every conversation.'

But previous generations had not been Evangelical
Christians, as they had what appeared to be a small
narrow cupboard and there existed an entire room
behind it. Someone came along from the University
once and told them that it was a Priest Hole. They were
barely two miles from Aylesford, which was a great
Catholic Centre. My sister who has done some work on
our family's history doesn't think the Priest Hole was
ever actually used. But it would have cost a tenant
farmer a lot of money and time to build a Priest Hole
that he did not intend using. Apart from that, if you were
caught with a Priest Hole in your house you could be
burnt alive at the stake, even if it was empty.

Edith was given a mug of warm creamy milk straight
from the cow. Then Eleanor took out a long toasting fork
and toasted some of her fresh, homemade bread on the
open fire.

After eating, Edith looked round. 'I want to go...' 'My
husband will light the lamp and take you down the
garden to the thunder box. Go to the boot room and get
your boots.'

Soon Edith felt tired and sleepy, so Eleanor lit a candle.
The older parts of the house had no ceiling and could be
seen soaring straight up to the rafters. 'Take my hand,
we will have to tread carefully. The previous tenants
took up part of the floorboards when they were looking
for a ghost. It's a bit dangerous, so your granddad has
had to rope part of the upstairs off.' (It was an old belief
that the ghost could not cross an 'empty space'.) 'Here
we are. I'll shake up the feather bed for you.' After

tucking Edith in, Eleanor picked up a large copy of the Bible and placed it in a corner of Edith's cot. 'This will keep the evil spirits away.' Then Eleanor snuffed the candle and bade Edith good night. Edith strained her ears listening for the ghost but was soon fast asleep.

The next day Edith was shown the farm and outbuildings. It was the Sabbath day, so Walter locked the piano, although organ playing was allowed. In the cellar were vats of homemade parsley and cowslip wine. Edith met Uncle Amos, who also lived at the farm with his wife and children and Molly the maid. Edith said what a dear sweet kind of old lady Eleanor was. But Amos laughed and said that when she was young she had and red hair, and a temper to go with it.

When Eleanor Elizabeth Brown married Walter Rolls Twort in 1874, she probably thought that she had 'done alright for herself'. She was the daughter of an illiterate farm labourer marrying a skilled craftsman, although her father had seen to it that his children could read. She came from the next village, which meant he had to walk 8 miles there and back every time he wanted to see her. He was 19 and she was 22. Her father, Joseph Brown, had married a widow called Patience Chapman, née Onions, but had himself been a widower for many years. Walter was the son of Walter Ballard Twort, a tanner, and his wife Susannah Rolls Twort.

Walter and Eleanor moved house several times, but remained in the Aylesford area where Walter worked as a cooper for Aylesford Cement works (barrels were used for cement). They moved partly because their family grew larger and also because Walter received promotion to foreman cooper, and that meant they could afford somewhere better.

State education was still fairly recent, but Walter and Eleanor became worried about tales of the use of the cane in state schools, so they opted for a dame school.

Then some bad things happened. They lost a daughter, Alice, who had been only ten months old. But their troubles weren't over. At barely 11 years old, their son Walter was rushed into Maidstone Hospital with TB and meningitis, dying a week later. This was the son that Walter had named after himself and was probably the child in whom his parents had invested most of their hope. Then Constance, who was 6 years old, died, followed a few months later by the death of little Winifred, only three. Both girls had had diphtheria. Eleanor was distraught at the loss of four of her children and couldn't stop crying. She heard that the drains around Burham weren't very good and pressured her husband to move.

They rented an old vicarage that was too expensive for the church on a mound at the end of the village. It was there that Amos, Annie and Valentine were married.

In 1911 another daughter, May, suddenly died. They had an inquest because she hadn't been under a doctor. May's death absolutely gutted Eleanor, as they found some letters she'd written detailing the books May had been intending to read and friends she'd been planning to visit. Eleanor was now convinced that the village was a death trap and became desperate to move out, and now she had grandchildren to think about as well. Then Walter found an old farmhouse that was available to rent some way out of the village, so they moved to Great Culand Farm and Eleanor saved the rest of their family. This was the farmhouse to which Edith was taken.

There had never been much of the Victorian young lady about my grandmother Annie, who was known as Nancy at home. May, Annie's little sister, had always clung to her skirts and tried to edge past rough village lads, but Annie always had a skipping rope tucked in the front of her dress and would yank it out and wallop them with that. 'That's how you do it, May,' she would say. 'If a boy fights you, fight him back.' Annie always felt protective towards timid May, and she too was upset by her loss.

It was Annie's job to empty all the chamber pots. One day Nellie saw one that Annie had forgotten and held it up at the window. Annie only laughed and went on climbing trees with her brothers.

Amongst Annie's relatives was Frederick Twort, a medical scientist. His son Anthony Twort has written a book about him called 'In Focus Out Of Step', and another cousin was the artist Flora Twort, who ran her own gallery in Petersfield, Hants. But Annie never seems to have met either of them.

One hot summer's day Annie had no money and so decided to walk home along a lonely footpath over the North Downs. Thirsty and hot she was resting under a haystack when a man came up and demanded money. Annie just laughed and said, 'I'm walking home because I don't have the bus fare, and you want money.' The man realised he wasn't going to get anything out of Annie.

At 13, Annie left school and was offered a post as schoolteacher. She looked at the headmistress and her two unmarried, thin and scraggy daughters who were also teachers and turned the post down. At sixteen she obtained the post of needlewoman at a boys' school in Broadstairs. When Annie came home in the holidays, her sister Cordelia had a bicycle and taught Annie to ride it.

Annie played both the piano and the chapel organ. However, her real love was singing and she wanted to be a professional singer, but her father Walter would not allow it.

The West London Mission following the anti-drink campaign of William Booth was organising a kind of Christian Music Hall aimed at keeping people out of pubs, and they employed singers. As this was organised by the Church, after much tearful pleading Walter finally said that Annie could sing and play with these people.

One day Annie was running down the stairs singing, and a new worker asked, 'Who's that girl with the lovely voice?' And so this was how my grandparents met each other for the first time.

The Mission's job was to try to save alcoholics, and they purchased a second hand shop to give an ex-alcoholic a start. This person had the same ex-army background as my granddad, who went to see how he was getting on. Soon however, Granddad found that this man had no idea how to set about buying or keeping books, so Granddad began to spend more and more time at the shop, helping him with it. Soon the Mission noticed and complained, but by this time Granddad had realised that vast profits were to be made out of the second hand furniture business and was thinking of a new job. Also, my grandparents' own family was beginning to grow. Then Edith caught diphtheria.

Edith went fishing and bird-nesting with her cousins. During summer they would climb down into the old disused chalk pits and gather tiny, wild strawberries. Also these old chalk pits were connected with a series of tunnels, and once they all wandered through them. Down in the tunnels they lost all track of time. At the next chalk pit they climbed up and asked where they were. It was only the next village, but they had believed they were hundreds of miles away.

It was chapel on Sunday, but in the afternoon countless friends and relatives would wander round (often unannounced), as country people with animals to feed couldn't really go anywhere. Everybody went straight to the back door and down the stone-flagged passageway to the kitchen. If by any chance anyone was out, they just sat and waited for you to come back. Back doors were never locked because it implied distrust of your neighbours. If anyone did knock at the door you could be out working around the farm and wouldn't hear them anyway. Once Aunt Cordelia came home from Canada, but Canadian homes are centrally heated, so she and her husband shivered and hurried home.

Another visitor might be Uncle Valentine with his two lots of twins, plus one girl, cousin Doris, in the middle. Uncle Val had his own orchards, but at that time farmers were in the thrall of the big retail companies. If Uncle Val didn't agree a price for several bushels of cherries they would send them back, and by that time they would be crushed and no one would want them. But what Uncle Val reckoned really ruined him was having to pay a tithe to the church (one tenth of his entire income), and he wasn't even Church of England either. Edith often tapped out messages in code on the wall to cousin Doris when they were both supposed to be sleeping. Edith didn't like cousin Len, who once put a worm down her shoe, although later he said it had only been a piece of stick.

Walter, used to being in charge of a lot of men, always spoke with a very gruff voice, and Edith was a little bit afraid of him. In the coopering business the men were not allowed to smoke because there were wood shavings around. If Walter caught someone smoking he would say, 'Well, I know I'm old and blind in one eye, but there is nothing wrong with my nose.'

In the country, nothing was ever wasted. Scraps of food were given to pigs or chickens. Old newspapers were cut up, threaded with a string and hung from a nail in the thunderbox to use as toilet paper. Cracked cups and saucers became flower pots. Dirty washing-up water was put round the roses to rid them of green fly.

One day Walter and the pony and trap were missing. He was having to travel further and further to buy food for his horses now that the first World War was beginning to bite. Eventually he had to have both his horses put down. Now Eleanor, already in her sixties, had to carry all her shopping home.

Edith's favourite uncle was Uncle Arthur. Home on leave from the front he would pick Edith up and swing her round. It was his death in Flanders in 1916 that really finished off Eleanor. Suddenly she seemed much older and then said that having brought up a large family of her own and now being arthritic, even with the help of a maid she could no longer care for a tiny child, so she sent Edith to the home of Eleanor, known as Nellie, and Bertram Cattermole, in Rainham.

Uncle Bert owned and ran a jeweller's shop, but his real bread and butter business was watch repairs. In addition to their back garden they had another totally separate garden some distance away, where they grew strawberries. Up in the attic they had boxes and boxes of apples wrapped in tissue paper, which lasted until apples came again. Down in the cellar they had potatoes in dirt trays, and they also grew gooseberries, black-currants, red currants, rhubarb, onions leeks, radishes, and so on. As the First World War progressed it became very difficult to get meat, and the butcher got hold of some 'rhinoceros meat', as people called it. People hated it saying it tasted terrible. The butcher said that they had to have it in turns. Every time he reckoned it was Aunt Nellie's turn she went up there and had a row with him. Eventually the butcher's face would drop every time he saw Nellie coming. So Nellie said they would eat only their own produce. They had three nanny goats and about twelve chickens.

One day the goats were sent away for 'servicing', and shortly after they returned they had kid goats. One of the nannies refused to feed her offspring and used to sit on it every time it went to get milk. In the end they expressed her milk and Edith was given the job of feeding the kid goat with a fountain pen filler. This kid became Snowy, Edith's pet goat.

My grandmother had said that she didn't mind Edith being brought up as a Christian, but she stipulated 'plain religion, nothing fancy', because Nellie and Bert were also involved in a cult. Joanna Southcott, a domestic servant, had lived in the 19th century and had left a mysterious box which could only opened if various conditions were fulfilled. But no-one could ever fulfil them, so they could never open her box. When she died, Joanna Southcott had thought herself pregnant with a mysterious 'virgin birth' and had made a lot of baby clothes, but babies grow, so some of these clothes were made to fit a very much older child. Once they dressed Edith up in some of these very old-fashioned children's clothes. Someone once whispered rather naughtily to Edith that in fact this person Joanna had had dropsy, but no-one ever knew.

Uncle Bert also did business with the Michaelite Cult. These people lived in a communal house with a couple called Prince and Princess Michael who, they believed, would never die. This pair treated all the others like servants. In addition to that there were a lot of tiny businesses around there who gave all their profits towards keeping Prince and Princess Michael. They had also been planning to build Jezreel's tower, which they hoped they could enter and shut out all wars, and so on. Some people called it the tower of Balaam (Bedlam would be a better word, considering what was to have gone on in there), but before it could be completed they ran out of money. They gave Edith a picture of what it was to be like when it was finished. They tried to draw Bert in, and brought papers down for him to sign, giving them everything. But he wouldn't sign; he was later to say that he picked the pen up, then saw the wife wink at him.

Nothing stopped the Cattermoles from attending church (High Anglican) every Sunday and taking communion. In addition to other things he was also a Freemason. Edith remembers 'egg Sunday', when everybody took eggs to church. Edith was not allowed to go to Sunday school because Nellie said that children on their way there knocked on people's doors, then ran away.

Edith was sent to a dame school. It consisted of about 8 children at different levels and ages that sat around a large table to do their work and the teacher walked round and gave each child something different to do. There was no P.T. – they just stood up, pushed their chairs back and did a few physical jerks, although occasionally they were taken up on to the common for games. On those occasions, gypsy children would emerge from the hedges to stare at them. 'Dirty little gypsy girl,' one child said, but Edith could see that if someone had blown her nose, washed her face, combed her hair, and put a clean frock on her she would, in fact, have been very beautiful.

Women often went up to men who were not in uniform and gave them a white feather, which meant cowardice. Even children did this. One girl used to toss Edith's hat in the gutter and shout, 'That's because your father never fought in the war!' Later Edith was to find out that her real father had been a professional soldier, and a very brave man who had been mentioned in military despatches.

One day Edith and some other children heard that a zeppelin had been shot down and decided to go and see it during their lunch time. They sneaked out of whatever passed for a playground, the boys leading the way. When they reached it, all that remained of the zeppelin was a charcoal shell and a dreadful smell of burning. The pilot's helmet was found two days later nearby. But while they were there they completely forgot the time and it was ages later when they returned to school. Fortunately their teacher was very forgiving and said, 'Well, it was the sort of thing I would have done, I suppose.'

Aunt Nellie and her mother-in-law were arguing. Mrs Cattermole senior had let a room to a lady schoolteacher, then had a soldier billeted to her. The two young people started courting. Bert's mother thought that an anonymous letter should be written to the girl's parents saying that she was consorting with someone below her class. The person assigned to write the letter should be Aunt Nellie. Nellie agreed to write the letter, but said that as a Christian she would put her name on it. 'No, they'll see Mrs Cattermole on it and think I've written it!' her mother-in-law said. Edith never found out how the matter ended.

Then the celebrations of the armistice started. The Great War, as it was then called, had ended. The year was 1918, and Mother was seven years old and was already with her third family, and her second school. What would the future hold?

CHAPTER TWELVE
Dumped by the Woman she called Mother

Edith now begun to think of and occasionally to call Aunt Nellie and Uncle Bert 'Mum' and 'Dad'.

Aunt Nellie had a long succession of maids. My mother Edith clearly remembers one girl telling her, 'You know, next year I shall be old enough to wear long skirts and put my hair up.' But when Edith met her about a year later she was wearing the now fashionable very short skirt, and had had her hair 'bobbed'. 'Why is that Alice gets half a crown, yet Clarissa next door gets ten bob?' Edith asked. 'Clarissa lives in,' she was told.

Uncle Bert kept a garden shed where his apprentices learnt everything they could about the clock and watch repairing business. The shed was heated with an oil fire, and on two separate occasions Edith saw the shed door suddenly get thrown open and the oil fire thrown out because it was fuming in an alarming way. One day, Uncle told one of the boys to light the fire in the shop and left him to get on with it. Something put it into the boy's head to use petrol to get the fire going. When he applied the match, the drops of petrol in the air caught fire and he must have spilt some down his overalls, because they caught fire too. Edith, who was 15 at the time, was walking through the shop on her way to school, and suddenly turned as she heard a cry. She rushed over, grabbed the rug and rolled the boy in it. Her action saved this lad's life but left Edith with a lifelong fear of fire, but neither of them ever told anyone about it.

This lad cycled through orchards on his way to work and started bringing Edith the occasional apple. When he caught sight of Edith he would stand up in the saddle and stretch one leg out behind him. Was he eyeing Edith up as a possible bride, thinking that she was the boss's only child and 'a good catch'? This was the young man who told Edith where babies came from. Aunt had simply said that 'God sends them' and had changed the subject.

Growing up in a shop that sold clocks, Edith would lie in bed and hear all the clocks strike the hours, some loud and tuneful. Sometimes she would try and follow one particular clock and its chimes all the way through the strike, but it was impossible, as they were so many different clocks.

Once Edith became convinced that there was a burglar downstairs in the shop. 'I'll go down and sort him out,' Uncle Bert said and went downstairs. He decided to pretend that there really was a burglar in the shop, and shouted, 'Come out Sir, you're cornered, it's a fair cop!' At one time Uncle was in bed, having met with an accident and broken both legs. Aunt had to serve in the shop alone and consequently had to close it for lunch. Then, she heard a customer banging on the counter as it seemed that the shop bell had gone. Then, when Aunt went to clear the windows in the evening, she saw that everything was gone. They must have broken in during the lunch time and disconnected the bell. They put the blame on 'the Hoppers', but Edith thought that the thief was someone who had been watching the shop and knew of Uncle's illness.

In those days, when stairs were often outside a bus and girls wore dresses, often only men went upstairs. Once they heard Uncle singing 'To Plough and Sow and Reap and Mow and be a Farmer's Bo-o-o-y.' 'Do you know that man upstairs?' The conductor asked her. 'No,' said Aunt firmly.

One day, unfortunately Edith was told that all the goats had been sold, including her pet goat 'Snowy'. Now that the War was over and food was more plentiful, Uncle had decided to sell the land that the goats were on. Uncle always turned straight to the stock market pages of the newspaper and walked, thought and slept business.

Aunt had at one time worn her wavy, chestnut hair long, but when she was about 21 she had an illness and shockingly, her hair turned completely white. Uncle, being a Freemason, said she had to attend 'Ladies' Night' and had to have her hair piled up onto the top of her head. Edith can remember her crying, so she must have been nervous about meeting Uncle's posh friends. Edith once said that the Freemasons were a bit like the Secret Seven, only on an adult level, and that one thing they definitely did do was to consume immense quantities of liquor. She knew this from clearing up afterwards.

When Edith was 13 it was decided to send her to a county school. Basically they were grammar schools, with the scholarship girls in the top class with the children of fee paying parents, followed the brighter girls in a 'B' form.

Edith can still remember some of the teachers. Miss Tesh would sweep into class, only a tiny woman, wearing her mortar board and gown. Even then, not many teachers actually wore them. Someone once asked Miss Tesh why she and not other teachers wore these clothes and she replied that other teachers weren't entitled to wear them. There was a horse running in the derby that year called 'Tishy', and this woman was known as 'Tishy' behind her back.

The headmistress, a greatly loved and respected figure, took them for scripture. One day they were talking about the book of Job and the headmistress said, 'Now all Job's friends came round, what for?' Some girls said, 'to comfort him,' others said, 'to console him,' and Edith said, 'to condole with him.' The headmistress said that 'condole' was a very good word, wrote it on the board and turned it into an English lesson.

Edith made a couple of friends at school, one of whom was Viola Cheetham, a scholarship girl. She lived a couple of doors away from Edith and would come and rattle her letterbox early in the morning. Both girls would get the three minutes past eight tram. Sometimes in the winter when there was snow on the ground, the trams wouldn't run so the girls would have to walk to school and made snowballs as they walked along. In 1926 the trams were on strike for a whole term.

Edith often helped Uncle in his garden. They had a signal, a chair on the lawn, and when Edith saw it she would get off the tram several stops early and they would have tea in the garden.

Nearby there was an orchard with sheep in it. If the orchard owner heard his sheep bleating, he would know there was someone in the orchard, and he would come to see who it was. Uncle got rather friendly with this man and tried to get him into the Freemasons, but they wouldn't have him. Although he was quite a wealthy man, he always walked around with his shoes done up with a piece of string. These small country towns were riddled with class prejudice and everyone was trying to get friendly with the people who were above them, including Aunt and Uncle. They knew a family who they believed to be very wealthy and would make such a fuss when these people were visiting that everything had to be just right. These people always brought a little present for Edith. Many years later, when Edith met them again, they told her that they hadn't been wealthy at all and often had to walk part of the way in order to afford Edith's present.

Most of the people that her Aunt was trying to become friendly with, Edith didn't like. Aunt had one friend, her next-door neighbour Mr Evans, a bank manager, and his wife from Wales. Viola Cheetham's mother was a struggling Great War widow with five children. Her eldest son used to make a bit of pocket money cleaning Mrs Evans' windows, but Aunt tried to break Edith's friendship with Viola, saying that if the Evans knew about it they wouldn't like it. Then Aunt Nellie quarrelled with the Evans because she wanted to be 'best friends' with them, but the Evans said that as a bank manager's family they had to have a lot of friends. Edith was disappointed, as she had liked Bronwen Evans.

One day a teacher, whom I'll call Miss Brown, asked Viola Cheetham to stand up and said, 'Viola Cheetham, I don't like you.' Viola simply said, 'Yes, Miss Brown,' and sat down. The next day she asked Viola to stand up again: 'Viola Cheetham, I've found out that you're a guide. I like you a bit better than I did, but I still don't like you.' And Viola said, 'Yes, Miss Brown' and sat down.

They learnt French from a real 'Mademoiselle' who used to get very excited and would stamp her foot and all the pins would fall out of her hair. The naughty girls would say, 'Let's make Mademoiselle's hair fall down.' On Friday they had games. The first girl would say, 'My Great Aunt went to Paris and she took with her a suitcase.' Then the second girl would say, 'My Great Aunt went to Paris and she took with her a suitcase and a handkerchief,' and so on, all in French, of course, until someone forgot something.

In the early twenties there was a great variety of sweets. There were great huge sweets called 'Gobstoppers'. Naturally, as a county schoolgirl Edith was forbidden to eat sweets in the street, as this was looked on with askance. But the schoolgirls broke this rule practically every day. One day Edith had just popped one of these huge 'Gobstoppers' in her mouth when she turned round to find the headmistress behind her. 'Goosh morthing Miss Broushton,' she dribbled, trying hard not to choke as she spoke. Uncle had carried a taste for cheap sweets into his adult life. At that time you could get a packet of sherbet with a big lollipop in the bag, called a 'Sherbet Dab'. Uncle rather liked these and often sent Edith to get one for his Saturday evening supper. One day, he sent one of the lads to the shop for him. It was really outside the boy's line of duty, and the boy didn't want to go, as he thought buying sweets was very unmanly. 'Did you get those sweets?' Edith asked when he got back. He replied, 'I stood at the back of the shop and shouted, "Can I have a couple of Sherbet Dabs for Mr Cattermole's supper?"'

Edith's favourite pastime was reading and this was looked on as a little strange, so efforts were made to curb it. Eventually she was forbidden to read, but found she couldn't stop. Without Aunt's knowledge, Edith silently removed every book from her Aunt's bookcase and read it, moving the books carefully up, so that they wouldn't leave a tell-tale space. For other books she simply borrowed from friends.

Aunt and Uncle were Anglicans, but her real father was a non-practising Jew. The two branches of the family didn't get on with each other very well. They were too well-bred to run down Edith's parents to her face, but once or twice, particularly over Christmas when there was a large gathering of friends and relatives, Edith had the experience of coming into a room to find everyone suddenly stop talking. What they used to say would go something like this: 'Well of course, dear Annie never moans, but we all know that Jack gets drunk and keeps giving her a lot of children that she doesn't want.' Maybe a bit of jealousy came into this as Nellie, Cordelia or Mabel couldn't have any children and Annie had fifteen.

When talk turned to politics, Uncle Bert declared himself a 'left-wing Tory'. 'Good in all political parties,' he said. 'I think all farm labourers should earn at least a pound a week.'

In July 1927, when Edith was sixteen, she left school. In her last school report she had nearly all Bs. One sentence I remember: 'Edith is a girl who expresses herself well.'

One day, her Aunt asked her if she would like to have a little holiday with her mother. 'You mean my real mother? What, to see her again after all these years! What is she like now?'

Excitedly Edith packed a few summer clothes, and set off for a couple of weeks with her real parents in London. Her parents lived in a place called Bell Street off Edgware Road. Edith saw what had once been a fine Georgian villa now had cracked and dirty paintwork. Her father's second hand furniture was spread out in what had once been the front garden. At night it was piled so high in the front parlour that no one could get through it and they had to use a side door. The kitchen (where they lived), once inhabited by maids, was cramped and dark. There was no sink, so Annie had to manage with a bowl and a tap in the yard. In the back garden was an old deserted church in which Annie used to practice her singing. The girls all slept in one tiny room with bunks, and her brothers shared another room. That first day back, her father cooked the supper and made blancmange using a saucepan. The black from the saucepan was still on the sweet and Edith couldn't touch it.

When Edith tried to sleep, the teeming bed bugs made a beeline for her and they dropped onto her neck from the ceiling during the stifling overcrowded nights. Soon the back of Edith's neck was covered with festering boils. She didn't complain, after all she would be returning home soon and as the hot days finally turned cooler, she felt a little better and there were so many places to see and new people to meet.

She wrote a plaintive letter to Aunt Nellie asking when they wanted her home, but there was no reply and the same thing happened again. As the sweltering days finally gave way to autumn, Edith realised that she had been discarded by her Aunt, like an old worn-out shoe. Then her real parents said that they could not afford to keep her, so she would have to get a job.

As all her clothes were still with her Aunt, Edith had to borrow from her sisters, but nothing matched, and she was competing with smart London girls for what few jobs there were. Edith had hoped to be a teacher, but had to take a job as a shop girl.

Aunt Nellie wouldn't have a pack of cards in the house but to Edith's surprise, her real father now went out gambling. In Rainham, when the hops were gathered in, everyone sampled the beer and lots of farmers liked their pint. Once in London however, Edith saw a drunk man chasing his wife with a chopper. She had never seen that sort of thing, and soon she found out that her father drank, too.

Annie had never had any regular housekeeping money. Granddad would give her a few shillings each day for the food, so she begged Edith for more and more money. She could never afford a hairdresser or sanitary items and had few clothes. Edith had no medical records, no birth certificate and no photographs of herself as a child except an old school photo which Viola sent her. The shock of being discarded caused her periods to stop for about six months. She soon found that there was no place for her at the dinner table, and that one of her sisters was very jealous of her. It was a long time, if at all, that she ever felt at home with her real family. Once Edith asked her mother why she hadn't been informed about something and was told, 'Well, I never really think of you as one of my children.'

Then Edith heard that Nellie had to go into hospital for an operation and hadn't regained consciousness. Uncle was lost without someone to look after him and asked a distant cousin to be his housekeeper. Soon after he married this lady, and they moved to Sittingbourne to be near her parents.

When Edith met Uncle and his new wife (possibly at her grandparents' funeral) she noticed that her own beads were now round this woman's neck. So now Edith really had no home to return to.

Even today, Edith can think of no reason for her Aunt's strange behaviour. She had had a lot of sickness prior to her operation, so did she think that she was at long last expecting a baby of her own? Or did she just want Edith out of the way because she sensed death approaching? Or did her real parents send for her, because they needed her wages? Edith was never given any proper explanation and consequently never really recovered from the shock.

My sister thinks that Mother's spirit was broken when she was a child, but this explanation has never satisfied me. I think that the constant changes from one kind of home to another gave my mother an identity crisis and this was why she was never able to put up any kind of defence, particularly when my father bullied me.

CHAPTER THIRTEEN
Amelia

My grandmother's story goes back further than my own memories. On the 21st of September 1844 a baby girl was born at 1 George Road in the registration area of St. Mary Magdalen in the sub-district of St. James, Bermondsey. Her father was a cooper, so he was probably attached to or worked for a brewery, although occasionally barrels were used for other things. Her father's name was George Bingley, and her mother was Harriet whose maiden name was Bennett or Barnett or Barret; the birth certificate is not too clear on this point. The baby girl was called Amelia and was my grandmother's mother.

I can't remember my grandma ever mentioning her mother except in very general terms, such as 'I was jumping up and down in the Airey and my mother told me to stop it'. An Airey was a flight of steps leading down to a basement. I know nothing or very little of her mother's early life. School was not compulsory at that time, but Amelia could read and write (or at least read and write well enough to sign her own name on her marriage certificate), so this cooper, who could read and write himself, must have sent his daughter to school.

As a cooper, her father would have been a skilled man, so they lived in one of the better parts of Bermondsey, not the rundown Jacob's Island end.

On 9th January 1875 Samuel Saville married my grandmother's mother, Amelia Bingley, at St. Mark's, Clerkenwell. By this time he had moved to 27 Meredith Street. At 34, Saville, a widower, had already been through a lot. He had lost three small children to a scarlet fever epidemic. Then his wife Rebecca had died, ostensibly of typhus, but I think she died of a broken heart at the loss of her entire family. If that wasn't bad enough, Saville lost both his parents around that time, when they were both still fairly young.

By 1877 the Savilles had moved to 34 Minton Street in Hoxton Old Town in the registration District of Shoreditch, and it was there that their first child Samuel, always known as John, was born. On this occasion Saville described himself as a butcher.

On the 30th of April 1881 they had a baby girl, who was also called Amelia, and she was my grandmother. Her birth wasn't registered until late in the following June so I'm guessing that either she, or her mother, was ill following the birth. By this time they were back in Holborn, living at Rahere Street, and this time Saville gave his occupation as a carman.

By 1884 the Savilles had moved to 74 Compton Street, off Goswell Road, at that time part of Hampstead (then in Middlesex), where Samuel became very ill and was taken into the North Western Hospital. It was there that he died on the 9th November 1884 of smallpox, and on this occasion his occupation had been given as waste paper dealer. He was only 45 years old and little Amelia would have been three and a half, and her brother John seven and a half.

On the 16th October 1889 Amelia Saville, the widow, married Henry Alderton, who was the son of a blacksmith. She did something a bit naughty: she told him she was only 35. She would in actual fact have been 44, but he was only 26 years old. I once asked my father why his grandmother had lied about her age and he said, 'Well, working class women didn't have much choice in those days. A second husband was an absolute necessity to a widow with a young family.' 'Yes,' I thought, 'But he had a choice, didn't he?'

The first photographs that I've got show my great-grandmother Amelia (who in fact looked nearer 44 than 35), and I've also got a photograph of young Amelia and John Saville. She looks to be aged somewhere between six and eight, and John, who would have been about 12, and is standing behind a chair. In those days you had to visit a photographic studio to have a photograph taken, and you had to pay them, so it was probably taken to mark some special occasion, possibly her mother's second marriage. Nobody seems to have a photo of either Samuel Saville or Henry Alderton and I can't remember my Gran ever mentioning either of them. As a young woman my grandmother had thick, black hair which, given that her mother was fair, she possibly had inherited her colouring from her father.

For some reason they moved back to Bermondsey (her father was dead by then) so maybe her mother needed a bit of attention.

At that time Bermondsey was the centre of the cake and biscuit making industry, and although Alderton was a stoker, he got a job at a biscuit factory. One day about three years after they married, Alderton was asked along with two other men to clean the top of the biscuit-making machine. To do this, they had to stand on something, such as a long plank of wood stretched between two ladders. Suddenly the wooden planking gave way. I don't know where Alderton would have been standing, but he hit his head on the top of the biscuit machine as he fell down and was knocked unconscious. Someone ran for Amelia and she went hurrying round to the factory.

An old-fashioned horse ambulance came and took Alderton to St. Bartholomew's hospital, but he died three days later without regaining consciousness. At this stage I know little about the Aldertons, but I know he had a sister, Annie Elizabeth, and a brother, George, who had been witnesses at his wedding. Victorian weddings were often small, but Victorian funerals were often big and they kept special black horses to draw the hearses. Maybe some of his workmates went to the funeral, and at that time people lined the streets and saluted when a funeral procession went by as it took the coffin to its final resting place. He was then only 29 years old.

No-one came out with any kind of reason why the planking should have collapsed the way it did, but the general feeling seemed to be that it might have been a knot in the wood, or the plank might have been stretched too far. I've since learned that scaffolding collapses were quite common in Victorian times, as they were not as safety-conscious then as they are now.

I don't pretend to know how Amelia managed for money after that. I should think her deceased husband's family helped her, at least initially. I expect his workmates had a collection for his widow, but I think that John, little Amelia's brother who would have been about 14 or 15 years old then, had to go out to work to help keep the family, and his mother eventually got a job as a machinist. As soon as Amelia got a bit older, I would have expected her to have had to help too. Girls could leave school at 13 then, but jobs for young people did not pay well. However the 1901 census shows that Amelia was working as a biscuit icer, and that John had left home either to marry or, possibly, enter one of the services.

One thing Grandma did tell me was that when she started her first job, she had to walk all the way from Bermondsey to Fore Street in the City, up near where the City of London Museum is now, and back every evening because there was no money for the bus.

I sometimes wonder what the effect of all this childhood poverty actually had on my grandmother. She certainly learnt how to economise, which is something that my other grandmother never really learnt.

When my grandma was about 23, she was working at a cake-making place in Bermondsey. One day her boss said, 'Here's a new girl come up to learn the icing. Her name is Susan.' Amelia and Susan (or Susie, as she was known) quickly became friends, going everywhere together. One day Susie gave a party, and what was more natural than to invite Amelia? When it came to going home Susie's mother said that 'now the young gents must see the young ladies home', and a young man appeared beside Amelia, saying that he was going to see her home. This was George, who became Amelia's 'steady' boyfriend, or 'suitor', as they said then. Grandma reckoned she had seen him before at church. This parted Amelia and Susie, who got a bit jealous. Susie was later to marry an American.

On the 1st of June 1903, in the parish Church of St. Anne, Bermondsey, Amelia Saville married my grandfather George. His sister Eliza and her brother John were the witnesses, and their first son was born in April 1904. By the time my aunt was born in 1909 the family had moved to New Cross.

In 1910 my grandmother lost her mother to breast cancer. According to her death certificate she was 64, but I make her 66. There are often mistakes in people registering deaths. Her son John was with her at her death at 17 Webster Road, Bermondsey. I only know at this time the bare bones of her life, but letters don't seem to be in existence and I have only the one photograph of her. Life gave her, and indeed both her husbands some hard knocks, yet in her fashion, she coped with poverty, and lived long enough to see both her children married, and would have seen at least two of her grandchildren. My uncle would have been six when she died and might have remembered her, but I never thought to ask him. My cousin says he never spoke about his parents, let alone his grandparents.

My father was born in 1913 and his brother Frank in 1915. Like most boys, they got into fights but were also inseparable companions going everywhere together and becoming fast friends.

On the 4th of September 1924 another brother, Alan, was born to the family. Dad would have been 11 years old and his mother 43, so this was definitely the last of the family. They were all very protective of little Alan. When he was about 13, my father worked very hard for a trade scholarship to a technical school, 'central schools' as they were called in London, something between a grammar school and a secondary modern. At one time he was top of the class for technical drawing, but somehow he seemed to have slipped back. Dad himself was to talk of difficulties in trying to complete his homework while his mother was bathing his little brother on the same table. Also, boys around the age of 13 often develop eye problems and something like that could have held him back. Dad didn't get the scholarship. One day he took Alan out, and Alan very much wanted to be taken somewhere on a boat. Dad told him, 'No, you'll be sick.' His brother Frank was always very sick on buses and trams. But Alan begged to be allowed to go and said he was sure he wouldn't be sick, but Dad was adamant.

Then one day Alan was taken ill and didn't seem to be getting any better, so they took him to hospital. Alan died on the 29th June 1931 of meningitis. He was only six. I don't think my grandmother ever really got over the loss of Alan. She talked about him a lot, right up to the end of her life. He had apparently never had any of the childhood diseases like chickenpox or measles. Now Dad wished he had taken Alan on his boat trip. Years later, when we went to see the film 'Oliver', my father was to remark how much the child playing Oliver reminded him of Alan. Something of the same eagerness to please, I think.

When Mum and Dad were courting his sister got married, and to my mother's great surprise she asked her to be a bridesmaid. At first Mum refused, saying that 'they've only asked me out of politeness', but Dad checked with them and said, 'No, they really want you.' So Mother agreed and for the first and only time in her life she was a bridesmaid. But unfortunately Dad's other brother was courting, too, and the four of them were often in their home together. My uncle's fiancée always brought Grandma some little present, but Mum could never afford it, and this led to a lot of difficulties between Gran and Mum as Gran got it into her head that Mum didn't like her or something.

Gran could be an exasperating woman, although not really a bad one. She used to tell Mum that she would be very pleased to look after me at any time if Mum wanted to go anywhere. Mum took her at her word, and arranged for Gran to have me when she had to go into hospital for two days. About two hours before she was due at the hospital Gran said she couldn't have me, and Mum had to put me into care for a short period. Gran did look after Tara and myself once when Mum had to go out for the day, but Mum never let us stay with her at her home after that. Every week she used to come over on Tuesday, then stay until Thursday, when she went over to her daughter's and stayed a couple of days with her. She was never an easy guest. Just as Mum finished getting us off to school, she would come down and expect her breakfast. Then, when Mum was doing dinners she would nip off. (Even when she was in her 80s she never once told anyone where she was going. If you asked her, she would say, 'Oh, around and around.') In the end Mum had to tell her that she couldn't have her to stay anymore, and after that she visited us only every other Sunday.

Dad was always trying to impress Gran with how good we all were. Once he put some extra lights in the back room and really furnished it nicely. He had also fixed up a series of bells everywhere. He said, 'After dinner I'm going into the front room with your Mum and Gran, and I'm going to ring the bell and I want you to bring tea in, with our new sugar bowl and some dainties on a tray, and it will all be nice.' Dad pressed the bell alright, but at the time Gran was washing up in the kitchen and was not to be impressed. When she arrived she would always ask if we had any books that she could read. By 'books' she meant magazines like 'Woman' and 'Woman's Own'. Obviously we had to give them to her and she would sit with them open on her lap while she and the other adults talked. The magazines came out on a Thursday then, and I read them when Mum had finished with them, so I was usually the one who was in the middle of reading something.

When the age of TV dawned it was even worse, as we always had to watch whatever Gran wanted on TV. Once for some reason I wet myself and Mum was furious because Gran found out about it. I think I've already mentioned the crying fits that I had when I was very young, but as I got older they turned into fits of hiccupping, sneezing and, for long periods, fits of coughing. Once I had an attack of the giggles (it was a bit like having a minor fit, I just could not stop) but Gran thought I was laughing at her or something, and it led to a lot of trouble. She always seemed to be behind me, always ready to run to my parents with tales.

She liked fish paste, so every other week when she was due over Mum had to go out and buy some. Nobody else in the house would touch it, and as Gran never finished the jar and they certainly didn't last a fortnight once opened, it would always end up going bad. My parents were on a tight income. Perhaps part of the trouble was that Gran really wanted to be part of the rough and tumble of family life, whilst Dad saw her as a guest who always had to be humoured and indulged, even impressed.

Gran was an expert and very quick knitter and knitted me some lovely cardigans and jumpers. She would say, 'And it's all in moss stitch,' which of course meant nothing to me. She also knitted socks and things with cables in, and so on. She could also make mats for the floor out of old rags (an art that no one does anymore, I fear) and as far as her means allowed, she was generous. She once gave me a bracelet made of jet. Shortly after I broke it. I practically kicked myself for it later when jet came back into fashion.

Once when we were out I pointed out an election poster that said 'Vote Conservative for good homes and gardens' and she said 'Yep, good homes and gardens for themselves.' I remember that when the Conservatives put some tax on food she turned to Dad and said 'At least Attlee never touched our food.' So I came to the conclusion that Grandma favoured the Labour Party.

I always supposed, until I looked into it, that my Dad's socialism actually came from his father and indeed his grandfather. When I checked with my cousin in Harpenden, she told me that her Granddad was not only not a socialist but not a Methodist either – he was an Anglican. So I thought some Anglican churches are very much 'gospel service' orientated and little different from the Methodist's. When I traced the church that they actually worshipped at, it turned out to be a very High Anglo-Catholic church. So that idea must have been wrong. Just lately I've been wondering if the family socialist was really John Saville, Amelia's brother. I suppose now I'll never know.

When she was very elderly and there was no one to care for her, Grandma came to live with us. She had her own separate room with her own TV and Mum would send up all her meals.

In the summer of 1965 she started going downhill and gradually became insensible of the things around her. In her mind she returned to the time of her life when she had been the happiest, which was when her children were small.

'Is it 9 o'clock yet?' little Alan would say and in her mind, and she once more went to the door of the house to see little Alan hurrying to school. As he turned the end of the road he looked round and saw her watching him and waved, and she turned to go back into the house. In those days people planted a lot of trees in their front gardens. 'People went in for it years ago,' as my father said. But this made the interiors of the houses very dark. As Grandma entered the house, all the darkness rushed in.

She died on the 5th of October 1965 at 84 years old.

CHAPTER FOURTEEN
My Nursing Days

As an Asperger sufferer I had the greatest difficulty in getting jobs, and if I got one I found that I couldn't keep it and lost it after a few weeks. With hindsight I can see that this was partly due to my inability to relate to any of my colleagues, and the fact that I was so slow in doing anything. Also, I myself soon got bored with various jobs, and apart from anything else, I wanted to travel.

Then one day I saw an advertisement for nursing and it said that you didn't need any qualifications. A girl I was working with at the time also mentioned that it was the kind of job you could travel with, and that eventually she planned to join the Flying Doctor Service in Australia. I wanted to travel too, and gradually the thought of nursing began to take root in my mind. Then I discovered that if I became a nurse, I would be able to leave home, and this was something I very much wanted to do. So finally, I went to the youth section of the local Labour Exchange and asked if they could they possibly find me a nursing job. I was very pleased when they told me that they had had a deputy matron on the phone about the possibility of getting them some staff that very morning. It transpired that they had a whole group of student nurses starting the next day, and if I hadn't joined them then, I would have had to wait another 6 months.

In England, January 1963 was one of the worst winters on record, with very deep snow. I was sent to a hospital called St. Gabriel's and the sister tutor there asked me to sit an exam which, partly to my surprise, I passed. These days you need a nursing degree but at that time it was just a few sums and an essay that you had to do. The sister tutor asked me if I could start there the next day, as she had a new Preliminary Training School starting then, and I agreed.

My arrival coincided with some National Health cutbacks, so they had just reduced the PTS from 3 months to 6 weeks. Some girls had been held over from the previous intake, as it was considered they'd taken on too many. We had two Chinese girls in my set, two Irish girls, a Dutch girl, myself and one other English girl, who also lived locally.

St. Gabriel's in those days was run by the National Health Service, but in many ways remained a Roman Catholic Hospital. The chief doctor, the matron and, I believe, her deputy, were all Roman Catholics and so were about 60% of the staff.

Lessons on anatomy and physiology started with bones. They had as skeleton (known to the entire teaching staff as 'Daphne') and we had to learn the names of all Daphne's bones. They had an entire 'mock up' of a human body that was made of wood, which we had to take apart and then piece back together, rather like a jigsaw puzzle. I would rush to finish putting the outer skin on the body, then realise I had a few pieces of body still in my hand that hadn't been put back!

My pay was 12 pounds and 10 shilling per month, but with that I was given a room in the nurses' home and all my meals were provided for me and uniform and laundry paid for. They even had someone to clean our rooms. So, in actual fact, I was better off than living at home, where I'd had to hand a large portion of my wages to my mother, and the little remaining was spent on food and fares.

Then they increased our pay, and of course the hospital authorities promptly put up the cost of board residence, so we earned 11 pounds and 15 shilling per month. As a single girl naturally it was great for me, but the few married staff didn't find it so good. At first I had some difficulties as I had to get a bag to carry all my numerous study books in, and my coloured pencils to do all my diagrams with.

In addition to anatomy we had a few lessons on how to lift heavy people. 'It's really a question of getting the knack,' someone told me. We had the respective doctors (or, as I now learned to call them, 'consultants') come to lecture to us. The chief surgeon, the heart surgeon, the psychiatrist, even the padre. I think the catering manager came at one time to speak to us as well, about special patient diets.

The orthopaedic surgeon was one I really disliked, as he was a bit arrogant. He would go round and start picking on West Indian girls and ask them questions they couldn't answer, trying to make them look stupid. I was shocked – I had always associated colour prejudice with louts in the street, not educated consultants.

My first ward was called 'Lesnes' and theoretically it was 'medical', but in fact, as I've already said, the winter of 1963 was one of the worst in living memory and the cold weather was just killing the old people off. Soon we had the ward chock-a-block with 6 extra beds in the middle. It was chronic and we were frightfully busy. The ward had a bridge and day room, but the day room was filled with babies and when you'd finished everything else you had to go and start feeding the babies.

I can still be shocked at some of the things that I saw. We had an old lady who had had a stroke and couldn't speak, but we found out that her son, who hadn't wanted her in the house, had pushed her down the stairs. But the most shocking case was a fairly young woman named Barbara with pernicious anaemia, who had bedsores so bad you could see the bone even on her arms. One of the nurses came up and asked me to come and help her with Barbara, but the sister came up and turfed me out, saying that this 'isn't the sort of thing that a young student nurse should really see'. A few days after that they transferred me to Elizabeth Ward, where they had a few children.

Shortly after I started we had a young Irish boy, about eight years old, brought in. He had fallen under a bus. He had cerebral spinal fluid coming out of his ears, and amongst themselves the doctors admitted that they didn't rate his chances of success very high. I'll never forget the high-pitched cry of a child that has been brain damaged. It had a dismal effect on other children in the ward, who thought that if he was crying, then they had to cry, too.

I remember one little boy called Victor, who was brought in at the beginning of the Easter holidays with burns. However it was decided that his burns weren't that serious, and that as soon as his mother came in, she was to be told she could take Victor home. But she didn't come in until the Easter holidays were over. Finally we began to wonder if Victor's burns really had been an accident. But Victor decided he was going to be a very naughty little boy. He had a model aeroplane which he'd got from somewhere, and he started chucking his model aeroplane about and somehow or other it always seemed to land on the bed of one of the children who had visitors. One of the mothers came over and said, 'Its alright, I understand,' and from then on whenever she came in she always brought a little something for Victor. Not as much as she gave her own child of course, but something. I think people who can do that are worth their weight in gold.

We were sent for cookery lessons for which we had to go to a nearby comprehensive school. A van would come to take us. On the last night we had to prepare a special meal and bring our own decorations and so forth for the tray. I can't think why they chose to teach us cookery. We were even told that unless we ever did any private nursing, we would probably never use it. But it must have been something general throughout the group, because they had nurses from other hospitals learning as well.

We all had to listen to the daily news. At one time apparently the student nurses sat in their sitting room and talked about the staff nurses and the staff Nurses sat in their sitting room and talked about the student nurses. They were trying to get us away from all that, trying to 'enlarge our scanty thoughts'. At that time the papers were full of Hugh Gaitskell's illness and we were asked why this piece of news was so important. But we had already guessed that in fact he was going to die. One of the senior nurses pointed out that Gaitskell had had bags under his eyes for years and this could he a possible sign of renal failure. There has been a lot of speculation about this man's sudden death since.

Perhaps I should explain at this point that after we left PTS we had to keep returning to the classroom for further periods of study, after which we would return to our wards.

Incredibly the Irish boy with the bad head injury made it, but one or two others weren't so lucky. Eventually the weather brightened up and I was sent to Vincent Ward, a medical ward for mainly old men. One day we admitted a youngish man who happened to be a rather large person who kept coughing up thick black stuff. One of the patients called me over and said to me, 'Have you read the evening paper? Look at this!' and I read that on that day, the fire brigade had saved a man trapped in a burning transformer chamber. The patient gestured to the man with the cough. 'Its 'im.' This person was able to tell us that he'd seen the fire and got as far away from it as he could. He was lucky though and eventually went home.

Some of the saddest cases were to be seen on the medical wards. A young man, only in his early twenties, was brought in with kidney failure. It was when I was on night duty that I found people were at their most confidential. I remember this young man telling me about how he had just got engaged to somebody, and he concluded with 'when I'm all over this'. What could I say? This was before the age of kidney transplants.

But perhaps the saddest cases I saw were those of sick children. To do 'children's' we were seconded to another hospital that had a specialist children's ward. One little girl I particularly remember, who was aged about six, was called Susan. She had a heart and kidney syndrome and her parents had been told that she wouldn't make it. The mother told me that she'd already lost two other children to the same thing and had miscarried twice. I can remember her saying, 'When all this is over,' meaning after Susan was dead, she wouldn't have any more children. However, whilst I was there they brought out a new drug which was still in the experimental stages, and both parents had to sign a special consent form. Susan was to have it every three days. Every third day little Susan visibly brightened, and finally the mother was allowed to take Susan home. Somebody saw them in the clinic and told me that all of Susan's hair had fallen out. But as a nurse you never hear the end of the story, and I often wonder whether Susan did in fact make it. If they could only have gotten her through childhood, they might have gotten her through to the age in which kidney transplants became possible.

Whilst I was there something else that was very unpleasant happened. There was a sister in the ward whom nobody liked very much. One of the things that this person did was to get certain children up after they'd been put to bed, which was very early in the children's ward, and take them out to the ward kitchen and make them toast and stuff. Nothing very much of course, but other children were excluded. Eventually a lot of people, some nurses, I believe, a sister, and a lot of the children's parents complained about this person and they got up some kind of petition to get her out. So she was sacked and went home. At home her father was a solicitor and he told her that they couldn't possibly sack her without giving her a proper month's notice or anything, so three days later she came back to work and I don't think anybody, not even the cleaners, was very pleased to see her back. It was rumoured that she'd had an abortion (before abortions became legal a lot of stories like this went round about patients who weren't liked) but after coming back she started writing around for another job. When I went to another hospital she was there, so I had to work for this person again, and I was very glad that I hadn't signed any petition against her. But the second hospital kept her and other staff under tighter control, so she wasn't allowed to do the same things there.

I became very friendly with the two Chinese girls in my set. Naturally I had no notion about my mental illness but with hindsight I can see that this friendship was partly due to the fact that they didn't use the idioms that I had such a job understanding. I failed my exams the first time but passed the second time round. I put this down to being very well taught, by just one person. Fortunately I passed my finals the first time.

Once someone taught me a lesson that I will never forget. I'd been 'specialling' an elderly lady in one of the side rooms, and when it came time to go home, I was just going to ask if I could go home when the sister came in. I was told off for leaving this patient even for a moment. 'Nursing isn't as exciting as it's sometimes made out to be,' she said. 'Most of it is just a hard slog, but we do have to give a little extra, don't we?'

One day we had a young Indian woman brought in. She seemed to be getting better and she used to get up and make tea for the other patients. They were on the point of sending her home, when suddenly her condition worsened and she was close to dying. They brought in every kind of specialist to see her, but nobody could find out what was wrong with and her. She was pregnant and her husband was told that she wouldn't survive labour. So they brought in an emergency caesarean machine and covered it over. They said that after about 20 minutes of labour she would probably die and they would do an emergency operation to try and save the baby.

Of course she wasn't told what this strange machine was doing in her room. Apparently they did save the baby and a relative raised it. I think everything has gone through my head since then and recently I've even wondered if she could have been an early case of AIDS. I know that 1966 was a bit early for this, but I'm sure there were a few early undiagnosed cases, and she could have been an Indian from Africa.

My real problems with nursing started after I'd passed my exams and was put in charge. It now became more apparent that I couldn't control staff. Shortly after I became a staff nurse they brought in a young woman with leukaemia. She was put on the drug Mercaptopurine, the only drug they had then that was supposed to bring about remission. But she became terribly sick with it and they took her off it. She had been given something for this sickness, so when I went round doing the ward report I asked her if it had helped in any way. She said, 'No, you can take the bottles away if you like.' As I bent over to take them, she saw the report in my hand with her diagnosis on it. Leukaemia then was a death sentence. I managed to get a doctor to her and she gave her a sedative, but the next morning when she woke up she started crying again. I got into a lot of trouble over that, as it was considered terrible if a patient discovered what was wrong with them. They said that 'it will kill her off quicker now she knows'. This was when I decided to leave nursing and until quite recently I dated the start of my mental troubles from then.

Dulcie Hall

CHAPTER FIFTEEN
Marriage

Most autistic people and those with Asperger's Syndrome do not get married. In fact, most of them don't want to. I wanted to get married, but I was ill-prepared for marriage. Apart from the manifestations of my mental condition, which included an inability to guess what the other person might be thinking (nonverbal communication), I had my parents' marriage in front of me as a pattern. I expect some members of my family will dispute this, but to my way of thinking, my parents didn't seem particularly close (as opposed to, perhaps being actually unhappy). They seemed to have different ideas about almost everything, and this lead to a lot of quarrels and disputes but, somehow or other, not one of these quarrels ever seemed to solve anything. My mother, to my way of thinking, always seemed to come off worse, and in fact she once said to me, 'In marriage there's a lot of giving in to do.' None of this gave me much idea of the compromises needed and the 'give and take' of a happy marriage as a partnership between equals.

I had never had that great stand-by of most little girls, a 'best' friend. My sisters were much younger than me, and although my mother did try and make me take them places, we never became really close, and in fact having them tagging along all the time caused me various problems.

Neither of my parents seemed able to talk frankly about sex although, looking back, one of the reasons might have been that I didn't actually get much time alone with them, particularly my mother, who had to work every evening and Saturday morning. On Sunday we had Chapel in the mornings and in the evening we often entertained visitors. In what little time I did get with them

179

we always seemed to be surrounded by hordes of younger brothers and sisters, and sometimes their friends as well. Late at night it was always, 'You run along to bed now, so your Dad and I can get some privacy.'

I suppose I was a little bit hidebound, but more importantly I didn't have any clear idea of what could really be wrong with me. I wonder if I could have told Steve that I had Asperger's Syndrome, would things have been any different? At the present time one can look things up on the internet and get hold of a lot of technical information that wasn't available in the early seventies. The chances are that, even if I had been able to use the term 'Asperger', it would have meant little to Steve, as it did to me.

Also, looking back, we should really have had some very specialised help. Years later, when I told a social worker that I'd been all through my childhood and two marriages without either myself or my family having had any real guidance at all, or any kind of evaluation of what could really be wrong with me, she couldn't believe it.

One evening in the dining hall at night school while I was standing in the queue for some food, I fell into conversation with the man next to me. He was a tall, thin man, fair skinned, blue eyed, yet with black wavy hair (typically 'Irish' looks, although I found out later he came from Tyneside). He told me that his name was Steve Ditchfield and that he was in his first year as a young teacher. Soon we started dating. When I first met Steve we appeared, at first glance, to have a great deal in common. We both hoped to become writers. Steve even said that he would cast a professional eye over anything I'd written, as he'd once worked for a publisher.

His speciality was poetry, and in addition to writing some of his own, he entered various poetry competitions. Obviously we went to poetry readings together. We shared an interest in music and went to open air concerts on Hampstead Heath and elsewhere. We joined a chess club too, although he didn't take part in chess competitions. We went to many art galleries, including the then current Tutankhamen exhibition. Poetry in particular has a small audience, so it really did seem as if I'd found a soulmate. On our fourth date Steve asked me to marry him, but at that time I wasn't sure.

I introduced him to swimming, horse riding, and country dancing. Other men would have been frightened of making fools of themselves in areas they knew nothing about, but Steve always seemed ready for anything new and seemed natural and unaffected. He said he would help me get over my fear of animals by having a cat. He always had plenty to say and said, modestly, that he considered himself to be a popular person.

I telephoned my mother and asked if I could bring Steve home for Christmas, thinking that if we did get married, then the sooner he met my family the better.

At my home Steve played chess with my youngest brother and seemed quite patient with him, so it looked to me that he had the makings of being a good father.

Steve argued that a quick marriage in the school holidays would free up money for us to save for a house, as we were both paying out huge amounts in rents for our respective flats.

As the wedding day approached, doubts and niggles began in my mind. Steve started turning up late for dates. He said he would be coming to my place straight from school but then didn't turn up till much later. He always had a perfect excuse for his lateness, such as he had been collared by some parents as he was about to leave, or that he had to go for a drink with a colleague, who had just resigned. Once he'd got drinking with some colleagues and they suggested going to a striptease club, so he joined them. I thought about all this. I wasn't always punctual myself, after all nobody was perfect. By then we were engaged, but he seemed a bit slow about buying me a ring. Plus the one making all the arrangements for the wedding, such as booking the church, increasingly seemed to be me.

Once we were talking generally about poetry and plays, and he said, 'I think I'm a bit cleverer than you.' Finally I asked him, 'Do you really want to go through with it all?' First of all he said no, then he said he hadn't meant it. 'I really do want you. In any relationship one person always cares more deeply than the other. What I'd really like is an open marriage with both of us free to see other people.' I now know that it was at this point when I should really have called the whole thing off. The result of this was that never once in our entire marriage I did feel sure of him.

Other niggles began to break the surface. He always spoke very bitterly about his mother, whom he said he was angry with for not providing him with a father. Also he didn't seem to have a good word to say about any girl he had courted before me, those being Ada back home in Tyneside, or Belinda, another woman he'd known for a long time. He told me terrible tales about his childhood, such as his austere boarding school where he'd been terribly homesick.

He also told me something that I found quite shocking: he had been homeless for two years and had to sleep in the open. He said that once you slipped through the system it was very difficult to get back into it again. Once you start living rough it is almost impossible to get clean, and your clothes become crumpled and smelly. Without an address you can't get a job because the first thing any prospective employer asks is, 'Where do you live?' He once said that the only way to get back into the 'system' was to do a small crime, because the prison authorities would always release you into a hostel and not onto the streets.

At about the age of ten, he had been knocked down by a car and had to have extensive surgery. This entailed numerous skin grafts. The human skin is a very sensitive organ, and when he came round from the operation he awoke in a lot of pain, but horrifyingly found himself tied to the bed. Nobody had warned him that they would do this, and as a result he felt a kind of 'mad rage' at the world from then on. Other things he told me I've realised with hindsight I should have taken with a pinch of salt, but the skin graft tale I've always thought was actually true.

Later on I read a psychological novel where someone had written, 'Never trust a man who tries to make you feel sorry for him.' I only wish I'd heard this advice then. Was I simply very naive as a result of my sheltered background? Or did we both mistake physical attraction for love? I suppose in spite of everything, we were just two ordinary people who wanted to progress in life and be seen to do so.

Even more worrying from my point of view was the fact that Steve wasn't actually a Christian. It had been dinned into me that I couldn't marry anyone unless he actually had faith. The quotation that had been thrust at me was, 'Do not be unequally yoked to unbelievers'. I thought and thought about this and finally decided to discuss it with Steve one day. He told me that he couldn't make himself believe as such, but he promised not to interfere with my faith, or prevent me going to church. He also said he would accompany me to special services like Christmas. So I thought, 'Well, he can't say much more', so I agreed that the marriage would go ahead.

To my utter horror, Steve turned up to our wedding ceremony wearing a casual jumper and an old pair of trousers. When he was out of earshot, my parents actually had a row with me about this disgrace. They seemed to think I'd put him up to it or something, although the truth was that I hadn't had a clue as to what he was going to wear for our special day.

It had been agreed between us that once we were married, we would move into Steve's flat and that this would only be a temporary measure, pending us buying a home of our own. We had a brief honeymoon and did as we had planned. When I arrived at his flat to start our new life, I found it perhaps not filthy, but at any rate not really clean, and Steve hadn't even bothered to change the sheets on the bed. He had been supposed to be cleaning the flat and getting everything nice just before we got married, but of course he had invited a few close friends back to the flat for his stag party and the preparations for my arrival had been completely neglected.

One of the wedding presents we received was a nice set of tea towels. One evening, to my complete horror, I caught Steve blowing his nose on one of them. He said he was sorry and that he thought it had been a handkerchief. Later I was to learn that this behaviour was a typical sign of his general lack of cleanliness. I was also to find out that he often slept in all his clothes and that he wore the same pair of socks for weeks on end. He had to wear false teeth from a young age as a result of his childhood road accident, and he would leave them in for days at a time. Once he even left a lighted cigarette hanging over the side of a coffee table and burnt it. He also burnt through several saucepans and kettles. He even left a cigarette to burn into one of our new sheets. He had to be 'chased' to have a wash. I was to find he possessed no underwear, gloves or even a proper coat. I tried to look after him more and went to the local market and bought him several pairs of socks.

In those early days, Steve could be very generous. He bought me a typewriter for Christmas and a wine-making apparatus for my birthday. He also bought us fitted sheets. Some things felt right and so I tried to tell myself that the other things were just niggles or minor problems that could be sorted out in due course.

Once, I caught a bad attack of flu and during the night I started having a rigor. Steve was totally unprepared for this and seemed to think I was putting it all on and showed me hardly any sympathy.

I often didn't know where Steve was. I would diligently prepare our evening meal, but often he wouldn't bother to come home. I tried to tell myself that everything would get better once when we finally got our own home. Far from healing the breaches between us, buying a house was simply to mean that our eventual divorce was even more drawn out and acrimonious. I find that very few so-called marriage counsellors will actually advise you to break up. Yet, all things considered, I think that was the advice we both desperately needed.

As a teacher, Steve could get a 100% mortgage but in order to get a house within our price range we had to move right out of London to a place called Patsdown, which was quite a way from Steve's school. We managed to buy it fairly cheaply within the price range we could afford, because it needed a lot of work to be carried out on it. It didn't have a bathroom, so we applied for a grant from the council to get one built and I agreed to put off having a family until we had one constructed. It is true though that in spite of our differences, we found we could indeed work well together in decorating the house. But Steve would not help me with the garden. He believed he could get a better job, say, as deputy headmaster, if he embarked on a further degree at night school. This he did, and stipulated that he didn't want a family until he'd finished that course. This plan made sense at the time and I agreed that a baby crying would not allow him to study.

Steve always blamed me because he failed to get promotion at his school. However, later on I found out that the real reason he wasn't considered had become clearer to everyone else except me, and that was that he had a drinking problem.

But I still had a lot to learn about Steve. One day he asked me what jumper he looked best in. I replied the red one, but he picked up a grey one. Finally he admitted he was colourblind. We'd been married about 18 months when I found that out.

Ever since we married I had been encouraging Steve to give up smoking. Finally he consented and did manage it. I knew how much effort you had to put into giving something up, so I was very proud of him, but then I noticed that was when he switched from drinking whiskey to gin. I don't know if that had anything to do with it, but shortly afterwards his violence towards me began.

One day he came home very much the worse for drink and vomited all over his clothes and messed himself. He told me that he'd been for a drink with some of his colleagues and they'd mixed his drinks.

Then came Steve's violence. Once day he smashed a glass casserole dish that had been a wedding present against the wall. The pattern would be that the next night he would apologize and say, 'No woman should go through what you've been through. Look, as evidence of my good faith, leave that cooking and I'll take you out to supper.' Once he spent £15 on a slap-up meal for us (a lot of money in those days) and promised me the violence would never happen again. Of course it did, but at the time I believed him.

One day, when we were staying at his mother's house, his sister suddenly turned on me and called me a prostitute. His mother, primed by his sister, took her side and this led to a row. After that his mother always wrote to Steve through his school and invited him to her home for family gatherings on his own. Finally Steve admitted that he and his elder sister Lily had bullied his younger sister Susan mercilessly, and that's how he and Lily had cemented their relationship. They had apparently been trying to use me in similar way to how they had used Susan on the occasion the argument broke out at his mother's house. He also told me that in his relationship with his mother, he'd found out her weak spots and played on them, making her cry.

Now I remembered something my own mother once told me: 'When you go to a man's home, watch very carefully how he treats or speaks to his mother. In a few years' time, it will be how he treats you.'

One of the first holidays Steve and I went on was to the West Country. Whist we were there, Steve suggested we go and visit his old boarding school. We managed to have a quick look round and in fact met his old headmaster and the matron. The school's silver cups were on display under glass in the main assembly hall. I saw one marked The Ditchfield Cup. It turned out that Steve had got into trouble at school and his mother had been up there with some money and bought the school a silver cup to prevent him from being expelled. So I was to learn that, far from being unkind to him, his mother had, in actual fact, spoilt him.

When we met and married I thought we had a great deal in common, like our love of literature and poetry, but slowly I came to realise that we were, in fact, intellectually poles apart. Once we were discussing the play 'The Doll's House' and I remarked that the play was very much a landmark. And that in my opinion it had made equality between men and women more likely. But he told me that while he had been at teacher training college, during the first year he and some other students had performed the first scene as a satire.

Once I made an appointment with Steve to discuss a problem at a future time. We were to have discussed it on Thursday night at 8.30pm. Thursday eventually came round, but of course Steve didn't show up. He told me that he liked being what he called 'a naughty boy'. But to me that seemed curiously like sadism.

Slowly, all Steve's lies started to unravel. If you love someone you're inclined to believe what they say, but once the doubts are in your mind they just don't go away. I remembered the time he'd come home drunk and said his colleagues had mixed his drinks. Now I started wondering if teachers would have behaved so irresponsibly? And what about what he'd told me about when he was living on the street? He'd said he'd had to do a crime to get out of it. But how come someone who'd been involved in a crime had been allowed to train as a teacher?

Slowly, I realised that he would say anything, tell any lie to get out of a tight corner, but he would leave others, like me, to take the consequences. As it became obvious to me that he had lied to me on various occasions throughout our marriage, I started wondering just what else he'd lied about. Soon, I lost all trust in what he told me. If he told me that he would be staying late at school because it was parents' night, I would ring the school to confirm this. I know I shouldn't have done that, but I began to want to know where he was and who he was with.

I think that it was when I finally realised that Steve was a liar that we really started to go downhill as a couple. I even found out he wasn't the popular man that he'd led me to believe after all. In fact it turned out that there were a lot of people who didn't like him.

When we had discussed religion before our marriage, Steve had always said that he wouldn't ever stand in the way of my faith and would come with me to any special event. We had a Harvest Festival coming up at our local chapel, so I reminded Steve of what he'd said about accompanying me and asked him if he would come along. I explained that a Harvest Supper, although it does usually start and finish with a prayer, in reality it more of a social than a religious event, whereby the church family get to know each other better. After I explained this, he agreed to come. So I went and bought the tickets. Apparently, Steve got talking about this to his mates at school and they said to him, 'Well, if you don't want to go, then don't. You've got to think of yourself sometimes you know.' So he came home and said to me that after all, he wouldn't be coming. Suddenly I'd had enough and now I started making definite plans to split up. I realise that nobody is perfect and that all men do something but, I suppose because partly of my condition, I found this kind of behaviour impossible to cope with. Autistic people generally find it neurologically impossible to lie and so naturally are very disturbed to find others lying to them. I find that I become especially upset when I find out someone has lied to me, as I have never knowingly lied to anyone.

By the time of our split, Steve told me that he'd paid off all the local tradesmen. I found out later that that too was a lie, as he had paid them with cheques that could not be honoured. He refused to pay the rates and water bills, although he was in fact responsible for them up to the time of the decree absolute in our divorce. He served the divorce papers on me, specially timed to coincide with our wedding anniversary. I remembered that once, after the initial disagreement with his mother, I'd written to her trying to rekindle some kind of relationship, but she hadn't replied. On one occasion she was supposed to be coming over, but declined at the last moment. 'She's cruel in little subtle ways,' Steve had explained, but now I could see that Steve was just the same.

One thing that has made me particularly bitter was that he always wanted me to put off having a family. First until we had a house, then until we had a bathroom, then, when we had that, he wanted to have a child put off until he'd taken a degree at night school. Then, to my horror, just as I was about to try and get pregnant, he decided to do a second degree. Finally he admitted that he didn't want children. I think if he'd really made that apparent to me before we married, I doubt very much whether I would have gone through with it.

However, since our divorce I have learned that he went on to marry for a second time and has had a child with his new wife. My bitterness stems from the fact that by the time I actually met and married someone else, it was too late for me to have children.

So one way or another, I wasted five years of my life on Steve. Sometimes I wonder whether he has found happiness with his new wife. Wouldn't a man who said that when he got to know someone's weak spots he would play on them in any relationship, do the same thing to her? Maybe if he really loves her he'll try harder to make it work. Several times I've seen him in the street, but he has never had his wife with him and I've heard that he goes on holiday alone. She however may not mind about this; I can't expect everyone else to think as I do.

I of course was no angel, and there were times in our marriage when I know I was in the wrong. Yes, maybe I did, as he said, put pressure on him, although I still think the greater blame lay with him.

At the time of me writing this, Steve and I have been divorced for over thirty years, yet I can still remember some of the things that happened as if they were yesterday. What have I learnt from my first marriage? I'm inclined to say that men will promise anything, but after marriage, things will be different. Also, most people who set themselves up as 'marriage guidance experts' don't really know what they are talking about. Women tend to tell the truth when they are talking about marriage difficulties, but men will always put on a brave face.

My advice to any couple contemplating marriage, even without my difficulties, would be to see as much of his family as you can beforehand, and let him see as much of yours. Watch the way he treats his mother, because in a few years' time that will be how he will treat you. If he has younger brothers or sisters watch closely the way he is with them, in a few years time that will be how he will he speaking to his own children. Get to know as much about each other as you can, although this is not absolutely infallible. People can put on an act for years at a time, but they really are bound to reveal their true nature eventually. I realise now of myself that I had a 'problem' and so it follows on that I was attracted to someone with a 'problem'. I wish I'd known what my problem was so that I could have warned him. But how many people back in the early seventies really knew much about mental illness?

Finally, if it becomes obvious after a few weeks that the marriage isn't working, then split up before you tie yourselves up with property and children.

CHAPTER SIXTEEN
Intensive Therapy Unit

I'd been a nurse from 1963 until 1968 and then had a break when I did secretarial work. During 1974 I decided to resume my nursing duties and decided that this time, I would work for an agency. I duly enrolled, and after travelling nearly across London to a job placement, I was told that there was, in fact, a branch of the agency near my home.

I made a point of telling the agency that I knew nothing about intensive therapy work and had moreover been out of nursing for some years and that intensive therapy had come up during my absence. I was told it wouldn't matter and that if I were prepared to remain for some time they would be happy to show me. So I duly presented myself to the hospital. I was taken to the unit and had to change into the long green gown and special rubber-soled shoes, which fortunately the hospital provided. The ward seemed a bewildering mass of ventilators, respirators and monitors that were all new to me.

The screens were above the patient's bed, the idea being that we could sit at the table and watch the patients whilst viewing the monitors simultaneously. However, some fool had painted the walls opposite with a brilliant white glossy paint which acted as a kind of mirror, so that the patients could all see the reflection of what the monitors showed. We tried to joke with them about it: 'Nice view with TV screens around your bed!'

The first time I heard the word 'ectopic' I wondered if I'd heard the right thing. At my last nursing job I had been a pupil midwife and the word 'ectopic' had always referred to an ectopic pregnancy, a pregnancy occurring outside the womb. Now I found out that the word in fact refers to anything taking place outside its normal sphere. An ectopic heartbeat is a beat outside the normal rhythm.

Every nurse was given a single patient to look after and I was assigned a Mrs Lazdon. She was 65 years old and, until a few weeks before, had been doing a full-time job at her daughter's fish and chip shop. She had come into hospital a few weeks before with a necrotic head of pancreas. This is an organ that we cannot live without and thus is very difficult to operate on, as the pancreatic enzymes digest everything they come into contact with. She had, in fact, had nearly all her pancreas removed leaving her a diabetic. She was recovering from major surgery and had a huge corrugated rubber drain attached to the side of her body, and from this bile-coloured fluid was continually draining with its vile stench. We put colostomy bags on this to try to collect the fluid, but the whole skin area around the wound had become very sore indeed. Under sister's direction I, and indeed the other staff, tried every kind of skin preparation you can think of to keep this area of skin healthy. But her skin continued to worsen as her condition deteriorated and she dehydrated. When I first arrived, she was allowed ice to suck. She said to me, 'Nurse, do you know I can feel everything I eat go straight to that bag.' Indeed she'd had some fish and I could see it in the bag, still in its fibre.

Nurse Wong, a Chinese girl, and myself removed some of her stitches from the main part of the wound. The wound was clean and we even allowed ourselves to hope that it would all heal up and that she would get better. Sad delusion; the next day the right side of the wound had opened and pus and bile-stained fluid were now pouring from both sides of her body. No matter how often we changed her dressings, five minutes later she was wet and uncomfortable again. Every time we moved her bed we caused her agony. She was now so weak that it was difficult not to drag her. On her wrist, elbows and legs were many bruises that were the result of the countless infusions she had had. Later on they were even to try her neck. Her backside was like a pincushion from numerous injection scars – both antibiotics and painkillers. I had to take her to X-ray and it was painful to watch her. They had to turn her on her stomach, and this caused her great pain. Her poor general condition made it difficult for her to co-operate. At last, the reports came back from the X-ray department and we saw that it hadn't been a success anyway. She was so distressed at the thought of another X-ray that it was decided to take her to theatre again. When she came back I could hardly believe my eyes. She seemed to be all tubes and drains, none of which seemed to be labelled. There was still a hole where the old wound had been, and soon pus and evil-smelling fluid was pouring out once more from the old wound, in addition to the fresh sites.

By now Mrs Lazdon was begging us for injections to end her life. She was now a stinking mass of bruises. 'I can smell it myself, nurse,' she said to me. Her arms and legs were covered with cut-down sites where a doctor had had to actually cut into a vein because he couldn't find a suitable vein to put a drip into, so much so that it was now very difficult to do infusions on her. The area of inflamed skin around the wounds had increased so much that it was now almost in communication with her bedsores. I could have sat down and howled over her. I wouldn't have wished that kind of suffering on my worst enemy. Some of the nurses who had been looking after her had become attached to her and now dreaded being assigned to the case, because they hated being a witness to her suffering.

During the night a blood drip in her legs started running into the tissues. A doctor was informed but refused to come to the ward. The next morning she had bruised, swollen oedematous legs. Soon a massive hematoma appeared under the skin.

The other patients in the ward could smell Mrs Lazdon and were all affected by it. They kept trying to pull us aside and would ask us, 'What's the matter with the old girl in the corner? Poorly, isn't she?' She now looked nearer 85 and still the frightful smell continued making everyone want to vomit.

As pus was still pouring from the old wound, it was decided to put a sump drain into the site. It was thought this would prevent the skin from being so sore. Again nurse Wong and I laid up a trolley and naturally I started to apply a local anaesthetic that was on the trolley, called Lignocaine. But the doctor refused to use it and Mrs Lazdon's daughter, who was standing outside the ward at the time, could hear her mother's screams as the drain that covered 2 inches of flesh was first inserted and then sewn in place with a thick stitch needle.

Incredibly, she now had six tubes attached to her: the sump drain, a 'T' tube from the common bile duct, one from the duodenum and one from the jejunum. At home that night I knelt and prayed for her death, as there was now no doubt that death would have been a merciful relief. However, when I opened the ward door the next day, I asked one of the West Indian nurses standing nearby, 'Has Mrs Lazdon gone?' She replied, 'No, can't you smell it?' It seems that she had almost died in the night, but the consultant had been to see her and had reduced her pain-killing drugs by half and had her restored with blood and plasma. I began to wish she had relatives who were really wide-awake medically and would go for the consultant and not sit and tacitly believe all his lies.

One day I got the junior sister on her own, and she told me that in fact Dr Nesbitt was too daring in his surgery and that she had seen about three or four patients really suffer like this before their end.

We went again to change Mrs Lazdon's dressings, and I asked her if she could assist us by rolling over and offered her my dress to take hold of. She looked up at me with sunken eyes and said, 'No more nurse, I can't stand it.' 'We can't leave you in this mess,' I told her. She made a weak ineffectual grab at my gown as we tried to turn her. 'Nurse, I'm going to pull all the tubes out.' I said nothing, knowing she didn't have the strength.

Along the site of the original surgical wound great holes had appeared where her stitches had been. Bile seemed to be coming from every hole in her body. As soon as we rolled her over, the other side of her body would start. At this rate it would take us ages to change her dressings, and she was now doubly incontinent. 'Let's do something about her poor mouth.' There appeared to be a thick crust of her tongue. I tried to brush her hair, but most of her hair came away in the brush.

'Is there anything we can do to make you comfortable?' we said, knowing even as we said it that she would never be comfortable again in this world. 'Why don't you give me the last injection, nurse?' Sister came out to the office where most of us were having our break and suddenly said, 'I don't know why she isn't dead yet.'

At last I went off duty. When I got home I sank onto the settee, weary to my very bones. The only thing I could hope for was that she wouldn't be there in the morning. I went back to the ward. A West Indian woman glanced up. 'My shoes have come back, then,' she said. It turns out I had absent-mindedly walked home in this other nurse's shoes. By now Mrs Lazdon was in a coma and in fact died that morning. Laying her out was a terrible business, as we had to plug every hole. I will never forget the sense of relief to see that, at last, her bed was empty. After her death her daughter refused to sign the consent form for the post mortem.

Death has now replaced sex as the subject that no-one ever talks about. But I think the general public should know that doctors do sometimes exceed their powers and are not always the white-coated gods that people seem to think.

As for consultant Nesbitt, there has been a bit on 'checkpoint' about him on a completely unrelated matter.

CHAPTER SEVENTEEN
UNCLE STANLEY

After my mother went home to live she had to get to know her three brothers. Her two elder brothers, my Uncle Anthony and Brian, were a bit bullying, fond of fighting, going camping, climbing and swimming, and so on. Uncle Stanley, the youngest, was a more gentle, shy, thoughtful, boy. In order to deflect his two bullying brothers, he developed a gift for clowning.

Stanley was born in 1920, but growing up in the 1930s with his father out of work and no dole meant that there was no way Stanley could get any pocket money. Granddad suggested that he join a church choir. Stanley was surprised; Granddad was always pushing the agnostic viewpoint, and in any case was of Jewish descent. 'Don't bother with these Evangelical, born again Christians,' Granddad said. 'A high church choir will pay you.' Uncle Stan managed to borrow a white surplice from the church.

Stanley had to sing at both services on Sundays and received about sixpence a week, I believe. In addition he earned extra when he sang at special services. Around Easter, due to favourable tax returns there were usually a lot of weddings, and Stanley might possibly be asked to sing at several in one day. This, of course, was when he really earned some pocket money. He had to attend choir practice, as well as practising on his own, but Grandma was a good pianist and singer herself and was able to help.

Sometimes mother went to the church, either to hear Stan sing or just to collect him. This church threw a lot of incense about and mother, not used to it, finished up feeling sick and would often have to leave hurriedly. Meanwhile her two elder brothers joined the army.

When war broke out in 1939, both Uncle Brian and Uncle Tony were recalled to their regiments and of course, as an able-bodied 19-year old, Stan had to go too. Both Brian and Tony were sent to France, but Stan was sent to Batavia in the Far East, where he was captured by the Japanese and was forced to work on the notorious Burma Railway. Grandma received a brief note from the Red Cross saying where Stan was, but no more.

Throughout the entire war no one knew much about Stan. Mum says that she always had a gut feeling that he would, in fact, survive because his gift for clowning would save him. His family did write to him, but Stan never got any letters. He says other men got letters, though. Apparently the Japanese told him that the Germans had bombed London to pieces and that his entire family had been wiped out. With no letters, Stan was inclined to believe them.

In order to keep himself sane, Stan decided to try and keep a diary. This was very dangerous, because the Japanese forbade it. So Stan not only had to write it in secret, he also had to find the necessary time, and the pens and paper. Part of the diary contains some Japanese characters as if, at one time, he had tried to learn their language. Or did he try and write it on the back of some official document that he received? The diary is handwritten on different sizes of paper, and it is full of crossings out and additions so it's not easy to read. Here is an excerpt from it:

"...We are very cold, and the scanty clothes that we wore were soaking wet. Our hair is lank and matted, our shirts unchanged for many days. We are covered with dirt and some of us have bled from beatings given out by our Japanese overseers. We are all thinking the same. How much longer will we have to carry on? Is it worth trying to carry on? Near by, the Padre is holding a small service. They are singing the hymn 'Come Unto Me Ye Weary and I Will give you rest'. The words seemed to mock us. There is no rest for us. We begin to huddle together round the fire for warmth. An assembly of starving beaten men. I bow my head in my hands and catch a fleeting vision of a bright room in which a young girl is playing the piano, under my instruction. She progresses making many mistakes. Her brother, good-naturedly makes sarcastic comments. Her mother, kindly soul, sits by proudly watching. Her father after saying 'Good evening' is doing his accounts…The dream fades…We are all waiting, waiting, waiting…"

Stan must have intended trying to publish his diary as 'War Memoirs' after the war. I have no idea why he didn't. One night Stan dreamt that he saw a man standing over him with a torch and saying, 'I'm going now Stan,' and when he woke up in the morning the man was dead.

Sometimes the men used to sing together and, of course, many songs were forbidden. One song they did sing a lot was the old Evangelical hymn which runs:

'For the line of Judah will break every chain.
And lead us to victory again and again…"

But eventually the Japanese banned that too. I have never sung that hymn without thinking about Uncle Stan.

We didn't rejoice on VE day as my Mum kept saying to people, 'What about the war with Japan? My brother's out there.' Finally, after the dropping of the atom bomb, we were told that Uncle Stan was on his way home. Stan was on a hospital ship because of his condition.

His records show that he had had two attacks of dysentery (passing blood and mucus), plus some kind of undiagnosed fever. He had had three attacks of Malaria. In addition to that he had Wet Beri-Beri (with oedema) and was also jaundiced and with leg ulcers. There are details of medicines and treatment that he was to have.

Stan told us that when the Allies finally arrived, they were all too weak to rejoice much. He once showed my mother a poem he had written in three stanzas, called 'The Prisoner' about a prisoner toiling in the burning sun and feeling so hopeless that he prayed for death to come. Each stanza ended with death, creeping nearer.

Another time they saw a very young Chinese girl running naked towards a wood, pursued by several Japanese soldiers. None of the men found out whether they caught her, or whether, once in the wood, she managed to elude the soldiers.

Amid the horrors of the Burma Railway there was one particular fear that Stan never mentioned to anybody. Stan had become a High Anglican but he was still Jewish by race. Supposing the Germans told their Japanese allies to treat the Jews similar to what the Germans were doing, he could have been marked out for 'special treatment'. He never once confided this to anyone until the war was over.

While Stan was away Grandma missed him terribly but when he returned, naturally scarred from his ordeal, her feelings changed towards him and she found herself complaining about him. This reached the point where my mother stepped in and asked her brother to come and stay with us.

Stanley had a girlfriend before war broke out, and she had faithfully written to us asking for news of him. My grandparents had always conveyed what little they knew. Soon after he came home, he went to see her. He had been away six long years and things weren't the same between them, so it all ended.

During those terrible years men adopted various ploys to keep their spirits up. Some turned to religion, others to communism. Three men that Stan had served with made a pact that as soon as the war was over, they would have a much longed for drink together. One day they did walk out of the camp as free men and went to get this drink. What they hadn't realised was that it was one thing to drink as bouncing, athletic young men and quite another to drink as emaciated virtual skeletons. So it followed that all three of them drank themselves to death. When Uncle Stan first told us this story we found it hard to believe, but I have since read countless autobiographies by people who had known others who had suffered similar fates, and I now realise this story was based on fact.

In some way that I don't quite understand, Uncle Stan was concerned in this incident. Perhaps one of the men had been a close friend? Often POWs formed little families of friends who looked out for each other and shared scraps of food. Or maybe it was Stan who discovered the tragedy? Or maybe the news of this event went all round the camp? Personally I really wanted to know more, but my mother warned me not to probe.

When Stan came to stay with us, he started drinking heavily. He had not done so before going to war. We all knew this change in him was probably his way of blocking out painful memories. One day my mother tried to tell him that he was laying up more problems for himself. Stan flashed her a look and she was later to say that he looked like someone who wants to answer back, but knows they can't. This look went straight to her heart.

Then Mother remembered that Stan had always enjoyed doing jigsaw puzzles, so she went round to all our neighbours asking if she could borrow theirs. When she had collected a few, she laid them out around the house on trays, half done. Later that day, Stan spotted them and, before he went to the pub, managed to complete a bit of one. Pretty soon he was scarcely visiting the pub at all. I can still remember all those jigsaws dotted about, although at the time I didn't know why they were there.

Once Uncle Stan showed us how to hide a bit of plasticine in your hands and then work it out. Goodness knows how or where he had learned that. During the war we were all encouraged to keep chickens or other animals. Our neighbour had rabbits, and one day we looked out of the window to see some of these rabbit running about on the lawn. My sister Tara, then aged about two, said 'Dog!' very firmly. Uncle Stan threw back his head and laughed at this and dated his recovery, such as it was, from then.

Stan had become very close to another prisoner, a Chinese man, and when he got home Stan helped him come to England. Whether Stan helped him write a letter, or told him where to write, or sent him the fare, I don't know. When the Chinaman got here, Stan shared a room with him for a time.

In 1946 my Grandfather died, and as a self-employed person – a shopkeeper – he had received no pension. That meant that my grandmother was not eligible for a pension, either. All her children helped her to buy a large house in Kilburn, where she let rooms and lived on the rents. My Aunt Sapphire, together with her husband and family, rented a room in this house, and so did Uncle Stan, who by this time was married.

Uncle Stan always went in for giving the younger female members of his family, including me, very deep, un-uncle-like kisses. Once my cousin Sheila, Aunt Sapphire's daughter, said that Uncle Stan had started tickling her and it got so bad that she couldn't breathe. Aunt Sapphire appeared on the scene and told him to leave Sheila alone. After that Sheila avoided him. Shortly after that a rumour went around the family that Stanley's sufferings had left him impotent. Nobody knew whether it was true or not. He and his wife never had any children, but it was known that they both wanted them.

Whenever we heard that Uncle Stan and his wife were coming over, my mother would say, 'I don't want anyone to ask Uncle Stan about his dreadful experiences in that camp. He will want to put everything behind him now and get on with his life.'

Later, through his work, Stan met another woman and left his wife. Unfortunately it didn't work out the way he planned. Years later, after much difficulty, I finally traced this person and she told me that Stan had told her that he thought of himself as drowning in a huge sea and that she was his boat for a while. She also said that when push came to shove, she hadn't really wanted to break up either of their marriages and had been horrified when Stan actually left his wife for her. He had never been able to talk to his wife about his suffering, but this girl, coming as she did from a different generation, was prepared to listen. She confirmed his gift for clowning. A short while later Stan heard that his wife had cancer. He went back to her and nursed her until she died.

In the early 1960s I became interested in the CND movement. I asked Stan whether we should have dropped the nuclear bomb. He thought about it for a few moments and then said, 'No, in spite of what happened to me, I would never had agreed to that.' So I joined the CND movement.

Stan tried to share his terrible memories with a person in the family who had been his special friend, Aunt Garnet. 'You would never believe the things that went on in that camp,' he said. But Aunt Garnet, who had had a breakdown, was a rather nervous person and said that she didn't want to hear about it, because things like that upset her.

I followed the war in Vietnam very closely and demonstrated against it. It was when deeply traumatised men started to come back from Vietnam that the Americans coined the phrase 'Post Traumatic Stress Disorder". When I learned of this I realised, belatedly, that this was what Uncle Stan must have had.

I wish I could have done more to help Uncle Stan but I was, and am, bedevilled by my own mental problems. I have never felt the limitations this imposed on my personality so keenly as when my inability to help others surfaces.

People said, 'Don't tell Dulcie anything, she's a bit mental you know.' I would like to have done some 'good works', but no one would ever trust me with anything.

During his later years Uncle Stan returned to the High Anglican community where he had spent his teens.

After his wife's death he came over to stay with us again, but, by this time, he had become an alcoholic, not even able to do as much as the washing up without a drink. Consequently, my father kept making fun of him. My mother strove to keep the peace between them, but found it all a bit trying.

Eventually, Stanley's body just packed up with all this punishment and he went down with pancreatic trouble. He had an operation, but I knew from my nursing training that he wasn't going to make it, and privately I gave him 6 months. I believe he did in fact live for another 18 months. My second husband and I were going to invite him over but, somehow, the time never seemed right and then it was too late. He collapsed at my parents' house and was taken to a hospital nearby. My mother sent for our relatives, and when Stan saw my Aunt Garnet he said, 'I suppose you'll all be coming now,' so he must have known. Stan died the next day. It was 1987 and he would have been 67 years old.

After Stan's death, all the papers in his room were taken to the Imperial War Museum. One day my cousin Maria went there and brought them back and that's when we found his medical records and the diary he had kept during the war. I just wish that more could have been done to help Uncle Stan and those like him.

Every time I hear someone sing the song:

'Nobody Knows the Sorrows My Heart has Known,
Nobody knows but Jesus'

I find myself thinking about Uncle Stan. 'If only...'

Dulcie Hall

CHAPTER EIGHTEEN
CND

I initially grew up in a home without a radio or television. When I was about 12, my father acquired an old radio that he insisted could be made to work. He took it around to all the shops, trying to find the spare parts it needed, but people kept telling him, 'Its no good, get a new one.' We couldn't afford a new one, so eventually my father got it to work.

Suddenly I had a new interest in my world and I started listening to interesting talks on the radio. I heard all sorts of exciting stories, which eventually led me into more serious issues.

When I was about 14 years old I listened to a very interesting talk about the effects of the atom bomb. It concerned a Japanese fishing boat called the 'Lucky Dragon' which had wandered, apparently by accident, into a zone where nuclear bombs were being tested. All the fishermen suffered exposure to radiation in the atmosphere and subsequently died. One man even went home and dug his own grave in his back garden. It was not clear to me then why he should have done such a thing.

I have never been one for horror stories or fiction generally. Why should I, when there are so many bad things happening in real life? Besides, I am not interested in lies and fabrications, and have always been a person eager to seek out the truth. As I reached the age of 16 years and upwards, a lot of arguments started at home. Both my parents were fully paid-up Labour party members and chapelgoers, so politics and religion together with music (in my father's case) and literature (with my mother) greatly occupied their attention. Arguments about politics, religion etc. went on all the time and far into the night.

When the papers suggested the widening of the London boroughs to include places like Bromley, I remember my father saying it was just a ploy to break up the LCC. He was in fact a great lover of the LCC, and his argument was that the facilities in London (that is under the old LCC) were better than those in the home counties. He said that every London borough had a swimming pool and that the parks were larger and better maintained (he had grown up in New Cross and possibly had Blackheath and Greenwich Park in mind) and that transport facilities and schools, even entertainment in the LCC were better than in Kent, where we lived. He said that St. Sadie's Park was hopeless and that the local hospital wasn't adequate (every maternity case had to go as far as Bromley), and so on.

Mother agreed, but she was more concerned with education and possibly the international aspects of socialism. Father's chapel-going came into it. For him, the words 'Tory' and 'Gentile' seemed to be interchangeable. He always said that the original leaders of the Union movement were actually Christians, and he cited the instance of the Tolpuddle Martyrs, who were led by a Methodist Minister, and of course there was also Joseph Arch, and a great many more like him.

Any kind of social situation was agony for me, because I was extremely ill-suited to make small talk. I'd be dancing with someone and they would be banging on and on about the latest pop star and I would say something like, 'What do you think about the troubles in Cyprus?' (This was around 1957 when I was 17.) Consequently, I was often laughed at and told that I 'took myself too seriously'. Finally my mother suggested that I might meet some likeminded young people if I were to join a political party. Later I was to find out that something got crowded out with all these intense arguments at home about politics, and that 'something' was relationships with the opposite sex.

I duly joined the Labour Party and then moved on to the Young Socialists, where I became the Secretary of the Young People's Group. This made me a committee member and in addition to that I was also the Young Person's Representative on the Labour Party Executive Committee.

When the CND movement started, I became interested. I had heard my parents and grandparents talking about the nuclear bomb and I couldn't see why the Allies had had to drop a second one on Nagasaki. I thought then (and in many ways still do) that the Japanese should have been given a chance to surrender after the first one (if in fact there was any case for dropping a first one). So I became interested in this campaign.

I took my little brother up to Trafalgar Square, from where the very first march to Aldermaston started. In fact, we even marched a little way with them, but hadn't made preparations for a long march like bringing a sleeping bag, so, after a short way, I thought it best to drop out (apart from that, my parents would have wanted to know where we both were). However, for years I avidly followed all they were doing in the newspapers and went several times to Trafalgar Square to welcome them back.

I became bored and restless in my job with every day that passed, seeming to be just like any other, and so I decided to seek work abroad. In the Autumn of 1962 I ended up in Italy. There I became involved in voluntary work which came under a vaguely 'leftish' banner. One day I fell into a conversation with a young man who seemed to have the same ideas on politics as I did. However he went away, and I thought no more about it.

One day, someone spoke to me and when I turned to my surprise I recognised that it was the young man I'd met in Italy. His name was Michael Haveringham. One day our conversation turned to our mutual interest in the CND movement, and to my surprise (and delight) he asked me to accompany him to the next meeting. From then on, I started taking part in CND demonstrations in earnest. Naturally, as a nurse, I couldn't go on many demonstrations or meetings, but I certainly went to as many as possible. Although my relationship with Michael was a bit of an 'on and off', I found I didn't need him to attend the meetings with me any more and went alone. I realise now in retrospect that until I met Michael, my world had been bound up in the rather narrow world of the chapel and evangelist Christianity, but Michael and his friends seemed to open me out into an entirely new world.

Lots of the people I met on the various marches were Quakers, so I ended up going to their meetings and lectures to find out what they stood for. However, with my family's involvement with music I'm afraid I soon realised that it wasn't the group for me. I also met a few Buddhists and attended a few of their meetings, and I would have gone to more but I found their message and teaching a little bit confusing, and the more they tried to explain it to me, the more confused I became.

Michael and I started going up to Speaker's Corner to hear the many different kinds of speakers on many different subjects. Some seemed to be deliberately ridiculous, but I did not find them funny. I don't laugh very much at things anyway, but I found it disappointing that people who had the chance to speak the truth about something in public instead chose to waste everyone's time.

In the CND, the Church of England was represented by people like Canon Collins, so I started going to his church, St. Paul's. It would have been better for me if there had been more Evangelical Christians like myself in the movement. There were a few Methodists. Another person I listened to a great deal at the time, who shared some of my ideas and from whom I learnt a great deal, was Dr Donald Soper. I soon started to attend his church. At that time it was situated in the Centre of Kingsway, with a great big dove outside it. Roman Catholics in CND tended to look to people like Dorothy Day, and when she came to England I went to hear her speak as well.

When I got home, I found I had the support of my mother, whom I sometimes sensed would have liked to have joined me, had she been younger. However, my father's preoccupation with keeping the Sabbath in an age of genocide and mass murder seemed completely out of step with the age we were living in, and now I think that this sort of thing can be a bit overdone.

From religion I turned to literature. I had always been very interested in reading and had always liked poetry. Now I had met a man with a similar interest, and I think it was really this man who introduced me to books of ideas. I started reading pacifist literature like 'Peace News', and many more books.

Eventually I became very interested in war and conflict. It especially puzzled me as to what caused them. From this point I decided I would read every book on the subject of the Second World War that I could lay my hands on. I suppose I wanted to search out the truth as far as I could. Someone once told me in conversation that I could not contribute to a discussion concerning the war because I didn't know enough about it. This person had the effect of making me very determined to set about reading every book I could possibly get my hands on concerning the war. I read all the books on this subject at my local library, and then all the books in the borough. I tried to get as many different points of view as I could. First came all the 'escape' type stories like the 'Wooden Horse' and Richard Pape's 'Let Boldness Be My Friend'. I went through the 'Spy' stories like 'Carve Her Name With Pride' and 'Odette'. Then I became interested in the more unusual accounts, such as 'I was Monty's Double' and 'The Man Who Never Was'. I now read about 120 books a year but in those days, I think it was possibly more. I have always felt it imperative to read the complete series of any given book.

At that time it was possible to walk through the West End and see war films at almost every cinema, like 'Cockleshell Heroes' in one, 'Yangtze Incident' at another. I also got hold of the memoirs of the main combatants, such as Winston Churchill and others. Then I read every book I could lay my hands on about the Holocaust, and finally I turned to anyone whose experience of the war was really unusual, like, say, that of an English girl married to a German, or that of a German girl married to an Italian, or an American girl married to a Japanese. This enabled me to form some kind of mental picture. By this time I had almost stopped reading fiction altogether, as non-fiction seemed much more interesting and honest. I also read more history, and finally settled on a preference for biography and autobiography. Sometimes it was difficult to know where biography and my war book collection stopped and the other started. I have 400 books at home concerning World War I and World War II. Once I read all the books in my borough on war. I then joined the library in the next borough and worked my way through their collection. I now belong to another library and I am working my way through that. It takes me 2 days to read a 400-page paperback. If I am absolutely engrossed, I will finish it in one day. I also have 218 biographies and autobiographies in my collection, and I am adding to them all the time. I now hardly read any fiction, unless it is part of a course I am taking, as my thirst for hard facts has taken over.

Another great interest greatly fostered by my friendship with Michael was a completely new look at music. In about 1944 I remember my father once remarking that no good songs had been written lately, and that none of the lyrics (he would have said 'words') made sense. He quoted some such as 'I've got a lovely bunch of coconuts' and 'If all the world was paper', even more recent ones like 'Green Door', and there was another one about 'We don't want to go home because mother's all alone'. Soon, however, all that was to change. First came the new love-songs with 'Come Outside' and 'Teenager in Love'. Then came Woody Guthrie and the folk music movement. It almost completely replaced the Latin American music movement which had been so much in vogue when I left school. Suddenly a singer would walk round with their guitar, singing, and the lyrics actually meant something. Most singers just strummed, but occasionally you could meet someone who played it really well, and even my parents were surprised at just how sweet and impressive an instrument the guitar could actually be. It isn't completely true that Michael introduced me to folk music, but we soon both became very keen followers of the movement.

When I was 21 my mother bought me a tape recorder, and I was soon spending hours borrowing records from the library and recording as many folk musicians as I could. Bobby Gentry, the Seekers (particularly Judith Durham on her own), Bob Dylan, Judy Collins, even the Clancy Brothers, Leonard Cohen and of course the High Priestess of the movement, Joan Baez. Suddenly it was a very exciting time to be young. I recorded about six of Joan Baez's records onto tape and played them over and over, and I have never ever tired of them. Recently I have turned to CDs.

Michael also shared my interest in hiking and the countryside, and we were both keen YHA members. We went on long walks. With him I fully explored all the woods, fields and marshes around Brystanton. Then we started going on long weekends, walking and cycling around Hertfordshire and Kent, spending the night in various youth hostels. We visited a pacifist community, then on the A40 near High Wycombe (now moved to Robertsbridge) and indeed others.

Another person whose career was followed by all pacifists with great interest was Mahatma Gandhi, and I read a great deal about him. Another person whom we pacifists took a great deal of interest in was Dr Martin Luther King. In fact, I went twice to hear him preach, one time when he went to collect his Nobel prize, and when he was invited to speak at St Paul's. I thought, 'Well, I'm off next Sunday, why not go and hear him,' so I did.

Gradually the CND movement became the anti War in Vietnam movement and of course I threw myself heart and soul into that. Needless to say, at the time I believed that I had fallen deeply in love with Michael. I remember one day him going on and on about his search for truth, when I so desperately hoped that he would propose. We seemed to have so much in common: both socialist/pacifist, both Christians, interested in music and poetry (always reading bits of poetry etc. aloud to each other), he shared my own outdoor interests, and he even worked in a hospital. He had been amongst the last lot of people to do National Service and had become a male nurse. This was something he wanted to continue with in peacetime. At the time he approached the hospital, the first lot of National Health cuts were in place and they had their full quotient of nursing staff and couldn't take any more on. So he was taken on as a porter pending getting a nursing job, which he never did in fact get, because he left before then.

Finally Michael said that he didn't want to get married and indeed never has. He always said, 'Marriage would kill me,' by which he meant going to the same job day after day and he wanted to be free, to just get up and go whizzing around Europe, hitchhiking and generally enjoying himself. Naturally I thought that he would eventually change his mind, but of course he didn't and in fact we had an on/off relationship that went on for about seven years.

Michael had long thought of joining some religious community, or indeed a community that was not religious. One day, knowing that I had some holiday coming up, he asked me to pack up and join him in an anarchist community for the duration of my holiday.

At that time the anarchist movement had no kind of formal beliefs or credo at all. It seemed to embrace people with all different kinds of beliefs. They were shrilly insistent that there were no leaders. They did have a general idea of decentralisation (they said too much went on in London), and so on. But they were really concerned with the individual doing something on their own. Let's give an example: In 1963 some people who called themselves the 'Spies For Peace' found out that some curious little towers had appeared on our landscape. Those graceful towers with their delicate trace work indicated (they said) the presence of deep nuclear shelters underneath and were there to provide shelter in case of nuclear attack for all sorts of important people. There is, or was, one near the Houses of Parliament, and we had been told that a secret location in Fylingdales Moor was to give the top knobs a 4-minute warning of impending nuclear attack just in time for all sorts of important people to get into these towers. Most of these interesting places were well hidden away in woods or even on commons.

During the march these people revealed where some of these towers in question actually were and diverted the Aldermaston March (or some of it) and went and held a demonstration outside one of these places. Simultaneously they also revealed the location of other secret nuclear hideaways. One was near Edinburgh and indeed there were others, near other big towns. A phrase they kept using always sticks in my mind:

'Every organ of the state has been provided for in these places (with the exception of the Church of England). Those who have built these places want to make sure that the state apparatus outlives the people. We want to make sure that the people outlive the state.'

Nobody ever really found out just who the 'Spies for Peace' really were, although over the years there have been several contenders. The so-called 'Spies For Peace' may or may not have been anarchists, but acting on their own like that was definitely the kind of behaviour that the anarchists would have approved of.

Basically they held to it that there were no rules to society (people ought to police themselves) and every kind of 'organisation' meant that they were, as such, completely suspect. Naturally this community had no 'house rules' as such, and I looked to see how this sort of thing actually worked out. They didn't really approve of things like makeup and seemed to think that preferably people should make or knit their own clothes. (I did in fact make a dress, scarf and blouse under their tutelage and knitted myself a couple of jumpers.) One man who was a carpenter had made some delicate wooden screens to go round his bed. Some of their beliefs have since been taken over by organisations like the Friends of the Earth and the Ecology Party, now called the 'Greens'. One man was an artist, and he got some very good commissions while I was there. A few of them had good jobs (one woman had an extremely good job) but most of them just 'got by' with low-paid jobs. Michael, as a school caretaker, came into this category.

They took it in turns to cook, and some of them were very good cooks, too. I was almost convinced by them.

Then the doubts started. No house rules and everybody doing their own thing sounded good in theory, very idealistic. In practice, things were a bit different. Nobody washed up, for instance. 'No rules' actually meant 'nobody had to', and 'so nobody did'. When they first arrived, girls spent a lot of time clearing up, then realised that they were the only ones doing it and stopped, and everything gradually returned to its dirty state. When you really got into it, most of them were there for a reason. One girl was a schizophrenic. This was when the mental hospitals had only recently started letting them out, and she was holding down quite a good job, too. Two men were homosexuals; one man seemed to be convinced that everybody else in the group was trying to poison him or something, because he did all his own cooking and used all his own utensils including his own cups and plates, which he used to go and hide somewhere when he wasn't using them. Some people had let their rooms get very dirty and untidy. One man had a TV hidden away in his room (so much for being a community). Somebody acquired an old broken-down fridge, brought it back to the house and spent ages tinkering around with it, finally got it going again and it finished up in the common room.

Worse still, they had all sorts of friends and hangers-on wandering in and out during the day (and often late into the night). Unmarried mums who lived locally often popped in for company and casual sex. To be an unmarried mum in the early sixties, in spite of all the talk of a sexual liberation was still a bit of a stigma and these girls often wanted to be somewhere or other where they felt accepted, no matter what they felt politically. Sometimes they were the respective 'other halves' of people in the community, and I'm afraid this led to a bit of theft. I'd hardly stepped into the place before someone took me aside and told me not to leave anything valuable lying around. Eventually I decided not to join them on a more permanent basis, but it was certainly interesting to meet some of these people.

As time went on, the entire Peace Movement began to fragment a bit and in the States certainly there was a definite bias towards getting a better deal for their black community. They were trying to get to and sort out a potential trouble spot before it developed into a civil war. A lot of people put a lot of effort into this, but goodness knows how much it achieved.

For years practically all my thinking revolved around the CND movement, and in fact most of my spare time. For a very long time I thought that as Michael and I had so much in common we were bound to get married eventually. One day he told me that he was looking for a woman who would really 'sweep me off my feet' and I think it was then that I began to realise what I should have realised long, long ago: that in fact he didn't really love me. Shortly after that he announced that he'd met someone else. The nursing world is really very small and I heard from one of my colleagues that the person he had met had in actual fact been in a mental hospital, after suffering years of sexual abuse at the hands of her father. I also heard that she lacked self-esteem.

I often wonder if she and Michael did get together in the end. Somehow I rather doubt it. From what I saw of Michael, I am by no means sure whether he could have coped with this woman and her problems. After we split I didn't see him again for years. Many years later, when the Pope visited this country, I was watching his televised visit, and to my amazement I suddenly caught sight of Michael singing in a choir in Canterbury to welcome the Pope. For all the years I'd known Michael I'd never once heard him express an interest in singing, and this brought home to me just how little I'd known about him.

I didn't make any lasting friends through the CND movement, but with hindsight and knowing more about my own mental condition I've realised that part of the attraction was that they accepted me just as I was. In this organisation I didn't have to face the trauma of making small talk. Perhaps I felt more comfortable with a situation that was actually 'about something' as opposed to petty social banter that I could never comprehend.

At one time I even contemplated a career in politics and to this end enrolled on a course about the British constitution. But I found that when I really got into the vagaries of British Law (as it applied at elections) and so on, that it all suddenly seemed too much like hard work and I didn't enjoy it any more, so I quit. From then on I was just content to be an extremely interested amateur.

I have never really lost my interest in the CND movement, but eventually I realised that if I was ever going to get married I would have to get out and try and meet other people and eventually after lots and lots of false starts, I did meet someone else.

More recently I have joined the demonstrations against the war in Iraq.

CHAPTER NINETEEN
MORAG

It was a Sunday morning. My husband was cooking breakfast whilst I was struggling to feed our two small children. Suddenly the phone rang. I shouted, 'Can you get it darling?' He picked up the receiver and I could hear him repeating the things after the person on the other end. 'An accident you say...' Then there was a silence while the other person spoke. Then my husband put the phone down and announced, 'Morag is dead.'

'Morag? Dead? What? How? Why? When did it happen?'

'You're not going to like this, Dulcie,' he said. 'But they think it was suicide.'

In 1980, with a failed marriage and a divorce now safely behind me, I had been hoping to start a new life with a new circle of friends. Someone suggested I join a West End church with a larger congregation and plenty of young people. I must admit that I had to give the matter a great deal of thought, as I was already committed to a local church and my background is non-conformist while the new church was Anglican, but I decided to give the idea a try.

In fact I started attending their young people's club which met on a Wednesday evening, and that's where I met Morag, who was behind the desk, taking the money. She was a pretty girl, from northeast Scotland, with the clear skin that some Scottish women seem to have, about 5'6" in height, with short blonde hair. She had a gay, vivacious manner and although she was only about 6 years younger than me, she appeared to be very much younger. She always had plenty of boyfriends, many more than I ever had.

In the following November the church organised a Christian Weekend Conference for young people in the country, and someone gave us a lift there and back. It was during this time that I got to know Morag better.

When she was younger, Morag had been courting a sailor and, I believe, was on the point of getting engaged to him. In seaside towns in Scotland, apparently a high proportion of men go to sea. One night, shortly after the men had been paid off, someone had come running to say that their was a fight going on in the bar room. Morag's friend said, 'Alright, I'll go down there and sort it out.' That was the last time Morag ever saw him, and his body was fished out of the sea three days later.

Morag of course had to get over this, and she travelled south to Edinburgh, where she got a job as a trainee nursery nurse. Personally I think that she should have gone on to do general nursing, as this would greatly have increased the number of jobs that she could have done. But she didn't and got a job at a fairly famous boys' boarding school as the matron. According to various friends, she had never really settled into any job since.

Shortly before we met she got a job as a matron at a large, fairly well-known girls' boarding school. She was due to start there in the autumn term and they paid her wages all through the summer. Apparently she thought, 'Well, I'm going to have a cracking job,' but when she got there, all sorts of difficulties arose. From what she said, it seemed that someone there developed some kind of grudge against her. She was locked out of the lavatory and other things, and after only a couple of weeks she was dismissed. After that Morag took brief jobs, like looking after an old lady, but all these jobs entailed living in, and when they came to an end she had nowhere to stay.

For a time she stayed at various hostels, first in Westminster, later in the New Kent Road. I advised her to try and get a flat, even a small one, and make it into a permanent home, then get a job at, say, a school or a hospital, and from there build up a social life. However, her argument was always that live-in jobs paid more.

Then I got a postcard from her, marked 'South Africa'. Morag had become a 'children's hostess' aboard a liner. Unfortunately most passengers now travel by air and the liner had to close their passenger services. However, Morag did get good references from them.

Shortly after I got married I heard from friends that Morag had taken a job in Cyprus. I was at the time preoccupied with my own concerns, as we were in the middle of buying a property and doing it up and I was also trying various fertility treatments in the hope of conceiving.

Suddenly I received a frantic phone call from Morag to say she had arrived back at Heathrow but had nowhere to live, and would I be able to put her up? I said yes and thought that she could have our front basement room as a bedsit with her own little kitchen for £20 a week.

The next few months were desperate ones for Morag. She was now out of work and found she couldn't get a job. Unfortunately it isn't possible to just walk into a nursing job – they need to check references with previous hospitals first. Nursing officers could be away on holiday and perhaps due to staff shortages they might delay replying. Unfortunately, she didn't receive any unemployment benefits for a long time due to an administrative error. Eventually she did get it, together with an apology from the Department of Health & Social Services, but not before she was getting harried by her bank for the £500 overdraft that she had run up with them.

This debt led to a trap that proved to be a vicious circle. She became so desperate to reduce her overdraft that she would take any job that paid well, perhaps knowing that it wouldn't last, but then when she did go after a serious long-term job, they would look over her employment record and think that she was someone who would never stick at anything. However, in spite of all this uncertainty in her circumstances, she never once failed to pay me for her lodgings with us.

I gave up one particular morning to visit the Citizens Advice Bureau on her behalf, but they said that they couldn't do anything, as Morag herself would need to speak to them. Morag then tried to get casual work with a babysitting agency. For doing this she received the princely sum of £1.44 an hour (this was in about 1988) and out of this sum she had to pay the agency 22p per hour. Most of the work they found her was in West London, which meant that she had to get the night bus home. I advised her to tell them that she had to be given a lift home, but she was frightened that if they knew how far out she really lived, she wouldn't get any more work from them. One night, tired and dizzied, she took the wrong night bus and finished up in Wimbledon.

When I heard about this I advised her to bypass the agency and go to a few places like Gad's Hill and advertise herself, charging £2.50 an hour. But I couldn't make her listen because she said that Gad's Hill wasn't on the underground train network and therefore impossible to reach.

Morag then moved out of our house, giving me a day's notice. Later I heard that she was working casually for Reed Employment Nurses, which was something I had been advising her to do months before. Then I heard that she had taken a job in Greece.

Eventually I breathed a sigh of relief to learn that she had finally found a permanent job at a hospital not far from where I lived. Apparently it was in a residential home for mentally defectives. A new chapter in her life had opened. Or so I thought.

Now that I was married and was beginning to put down roots in the East End of London, we decided to attend a local church. After some time we decided to revisit our old church in the West End, and on that occasion we ran into Morag, who still attended there. She was with Rosetta, a young West Indian woman, who was a colleague at the hospital.

About three years later I got a surprise phone call from her. The home that she worked for had brought in long stretches of duty. She apparently worked all day in the hospital, then was on call all the following night. Then she came off and went to another hospital, where she slept. Morag told me she was finding the job a dreadful strain and very, very tiring. She said that after coming off duty after the 24-hour shift there was a lot of noise in the nurses' home during the day, and this was making if difficult for her to sleep. She spent all her free time trying to get other jobs, but a depression was beginning to kick in as fresh attempts to find alternative employment proved unsuccessful.

A few days later, while I was in Upton Park, I called in at a cafe and ran into Rosetta. I asked after Morag, only to be told that she and Morag were no longer friendly, as Morag was finding it difficult to sleep and was always complaining about the noise. She finished by saying that she thought Morag was a 'mad woman'.

By this time I was waiting for my husband to return with our other adopted child, a little boy. While I was waiting for him to come home I received another frantic call from Morag. She told me that her boss had managed to get her sectioned and sent to a mental hospital in the East End. She was on a locked ward and felt absolutely desperate. She asked if I could do something to get her out. While she was on the phone my husband came in with our second baby, who was yelling his head off with hunger, so I had to end the phone call to feed him. I felt bad asking Morag to ring off, but promised I would try to do something for her over the next few days.

I was at the busiest time I had ever been in my life because my children were so close in age and both under a year old. Anyone who has ever lived with a young baby knows that during the first few weeks they keep you awake half the night. My little girl, who was only eleven months old, also needed a lot of attention. I once calculated that it took me a good two hours just to get them up in the morning, feed them, bath and change them and take them to playgroup. In addition to that both children needed a lot of medical care, my little girl because of her tiny birth size and my little boy because of his bouts of asthma. So Morag and the desperation of her situation was put to one side.

Then I heard from Rosetta again, who told me that she had been to see Morag in the mental hospital. She said she had been appalled at the state she found her in and consequently had cried all the way home.

Morag contacted a lot of people during those dark months while she was incarcerated, and some of them had rallied round and managed to give evidence before a tribunal that eventually granted her release. Another friend of Morag's, a teacher from North East London called Suzanne, offered to put Morag up in her house.

A short time after this, when my eldest child was roughly aged two – this was in 1993 – Morag rang me again and asked if she could come back to her lodgings with us, as she wanted to return to the East End, where she had lots of friends. There were several new problems with this suggestion this time, though.

Firstly, there had been a certain amount of tension between Morag and my husband last time round. Then, since she last lived with us my husband had been made redundant and we had invested a lot of his redundancy money in doing up the flat, which we were now able to let as self-contained accommodation. As I had left work to look after my children, letting the flat was to be part of our income and we decided to charge £50 a week rent for it. Indeed, I had made curtains myself to match the furnishings. She said the rent we were now charging was not out of her reach.

By now Morag had a new boyfriend called Donald. Like Morag he was a member of the Church of Scotland, and he came from the same part of Scotland as herself. I know that this time Morag was definitely hoping that this relationship would lead to marriage. The only problem was that Donald, who was 31 at the time, was about ten years younger than Morag. Eventually they both came round to see the flat, and arrangements were made for Morag to move in. My husband was to go to Hillingdon the following Sunday to transport her bicycle in his car, plus any other heavy luggage that she happened to have.

Then one night our baby son kept me awake half the night and by the next morning I felt completely drained of energy. My husband kindly offered to see to the children and took them both downstairs so that I could get a little more sleep. When I eventually joined my family downstairs my husband said we had heard further from Morag. This time she said that Hillingdon Social Services had refused to pay the £50 a week for her accommodation, and that she would not now be able to move in after all.

If that wasn't bad enough, someone, possibly Suzanne, had told her that Donald wasn't really interested in marriage and that she should come to terms with the fact that she probably would not get married, and that Suzanne was prepared to offer her a permanent home for the rest of her life. At the time my husband was trying desperately hard to give two small children their breakfast and finished up being a bit brusque with her, something he was later to bitterly regret.

Suzanne's offer of a permanent home was not exactly problem-free either. Suzanne had had to give up her teaching job in order to look after her elderly, invalid father, so in order to keep herself, Suzanne had started giving children remedial lessons from her own home. This entailed a lot of weekend and evening work for Suzanne.

That particular Saturday Suzanne had woken early – Morag herself was always an early riser – and given Morag breakfast, which she had eaten heartily. Then Suzanne's children had started arriving and Suzanne had to turn her attention to them. After that, they both had had an early lunch and Suzanne noted that Morag had even asked for a second helping of rhubarb crumble and custard. Morag then left the house, saying she might be visiting a few people in the East End near her former home, and possibly try to get her old job back. By 10pm the police went to Suzanne's home to say that Morag's dead body had been found lying beside the track at Potter's Bar, with a one way ticket to Edinburgh in her pocket. Her handbag was still on the train.

No-one can really account for Morag's last few hours on this earth. Her death can be timed at 3.40pm, so it seems unlikely that she really did come to the East End and she may have wandered around the centre of London for a couple of hours before deciding to the rest of her fate. She must have concluded that at the age of forty plus, with no proper home (to this day I don't know why she didn't want to accept Suzanne's offer of a permanent home), no proper job in sight and no husband, that everything was beginning to really grind to a halt for her.

At the time, Morag had been absolutely adamant that her boyfriend Donald was not to be told that she was in a mental hospital. But if she dropped out of his life for several months and then returned with a barely credible tale about staying with friends in the country, I am not terribly surprised that he hesitated about mentioning marriage. After a long absence, a courtship would really have had to go back to the beginning again, and he could by this time have been involved with someone else. As it happened it seems that he wasn't.

Her face must have been badly mangled because the police found it impossible to establish her identity through dental records and had to go to Suzanne's place to fingerprint her room. For some time the police wouldn't issue a death certificate and without it the vicar couldn't conduct the funeral service.

I wrote Morag's brother a letter which I found very difficult to compose- I wrote how much I'd liked her and tried to be positive about her life and the good things that she'd done. I don't know if I put my foot in it in some way, because he never replied.

It has now emerged that, in fact, Morag's father had committed suicide many years ago, and that Morag had tried to commit suicide in some bizarre way before, but neither of these facts were known to either Suzanne or myself. I have subsequently read in the local paper that two of Morag's colleagues were accused of embezzling a patient's money, and they too committed suicide before the case came to court. I will never know how well Morag knew these people, but she had worked with them and this action of theirs must have triggered something off in her own mind. Another strange similarity was that a young person, whom she knew through her church and was also out of work, had committed suicide about ten days before. I also found out that shortly before her death Morag had been mugged in the street.

I find it barely credible that Morag should have been expected to work for a stretch of 24 hours at a time, even if for the last twelve hours she was merely on call. And as the conscientious woman that Morag was, she would have answered every call, too.

I wondered if she belonged to a trade union at all. There would seem to be several that she could have been in, such as NUPE (National Union of Public Employees) or COHSE (Confederation of Health Service Employees). Or she could even have been a member of the Royal College of Nursing. Unfortunately, without knowing the name of the hospital she trained at, or the date she qualified or her registration number, it seems difficult to find out whether she was involved in them. Also, I have very little proof of the long hours Morag had been working. I would need to know, for instance, when she went on duty and when she came off and some dates. On the other hand, if this human being really was harried to her death, surely it should be a matter for the union, whether she was a member or not.

How was it that someone she worked for was able to get her admitted to a mental hospital so easily? Apparently it was simply because he had a grudge against her. I spoke to a neighbour who is a psychiatric nurse and he confirmed that unfortunately, it is possible for someone with the right contacts to work the system to their own advantage, and it happens all too frequently.

Also, how did it happen that Morag was put on a locked ward? As I had always understood it, you could not be placed on locked ward unless you were actually violent, either to yourself or others. I realise that there is no chance that I could ever be allowed access to her case notes to find out how these decisions came about, but I did wonder if I could have taken the matter up with MIND, the organisation set up to help the mentally ill.

The inquest into her death was opened, then adjourned. I sent my one black skirt to the cleaners and arranged with someone living nearby to look after my children so that I could attend the funeral. I had said that there were various matters I wanted to raise at the inquest, but the family begged me not to. I was told that her brother had been through so much already that he couldn't face anything more.

Of course Morag had a run of bad luck, and in some ways was her own worst enemy. If her aim in life was to get married, then she really should have applied for a council flat ages before. She really would have needed to stay in one place so that she could get to know people. She should have forgotten all about jobs in Cyprus, Greece and South Africa. It was also, I think, a mistake not to tell Donald where she had been detained. After all, if she really had got involved with him, he was bound to find out in the end anyway.

Morag's brother Robin said that he could have bought her a flat in either Edinburgh or Glasgow, but he couldn't have matched London prices. This must have been some time ago, as he's out of work himself now. He and his wife said that she could have moved in with them any time she liked, but there were no jobs anywhere round where they lived that she could have done. Apart from this, she needed her own place.

The funeral itself was an informal service and the vicar tried hard to speak warmly about her, stressing the positive sides of her life, her kindness and humanity. Before the service, they draped a Scottish flag over the altar, which I thought was a very nice gesture. Apparently the man who was largely responsible for putting her in the mental hospital actually attended the funeral and sat at the back. Rosetta pointed him out me, but he disappeared rather quickly afterwards.

As the coffin went past, and I realised that her remains were in it and that her beautiful face had been mangled forever. I wanted to cry. It struck me then that even I had failed Morag. When she said that Hillingdon Social Services would not meet £50 per week, I should have phoned her back and suggested she should pay what she could afford and perhaps pay us the rest in housework or babysitting favours. But these ideas were not well thought out at the time, and now it is too late.

I contacted Suzanne subsequently, but she said that the only way she could cope with it was to forget about it completely. Someone to come out of it really badly was Donald, who is still unmarried ten years later. The inquest was finally held about a year later, but it was only concerned with the circumstances of her death, and nothing fresh emerged about her motives. I phoned her psychiatrist and told him that I was finding it very hard to come to terms with her death, especially as most people had been convinced she was getting better. He told me that when a person is really, down they don't have the energy to do anything. It's when they are getting better that tragedy strikes.

One day I was casually glancing through my old photograph album and came across a picture of my daughter, taken while she was a baby. In the picture she is wearing a tiny tartan dress with a small white silk-embroidered collar with tiny blue embroidered flowers on it. A friend had remarked at the time that it was a very pretty dress. Then I remembered that it was in fact Morag who had given me the dress for my daughter and everything came flooding back. Even now, so many years later, I can still feel an upsurge of grief at the tragic outcome of my friend's life. Perhaps we still don't know enough about mental illness to make any kind of judgement.

Dulcie Hall

CHAPTER TWENTY
Tracey

'Goodbye. Do keep in touch.' We had just returned to Heathrow after adopting a baby from the Far East. Another couple, Tracey and Michael O'Halloran with their 12-year-old daughter Patricia had also adopted with us. Whilst we had a little girl, whom we called Rosamund, they had a boy called Brendon.

Naturally, we had to pay the lawyer who had arranged the adoption and we paid her with a credit card, but the O'Halloran's had changed £3,000 into rupees. However the lawyer would only accept sterling, and they were not allowed to change their money back. So what to do with it? Well, we were planning to go out there again to adopt another child, so they gave the money to us. At that time we didn't have £3,000 hanging around in the bank, so we accepted the rupees with the arrangement that we would pay the O'Hallorans back in instalments.

Back home Rosamund wouldn't take any feeds and was admitted to hospital 10 days later. Finally they settled the matter by putting her back on soya milk. A short time after that we found out the real reason for all her misery had been that she had scabies. This is a common problem with babies who have been in Third World orphanages, where conditions are still a bit grim.

At birth Rosamund was only 4 lbs, although she had been a full-term baby, which meant that she had to have countless checks from paediatricians, health visitors, and so on.

A short time after we'd adopted Rosamund she developed gastroenteritis, and I asked Tracey to help me. She had more experience with babies than me, as she had brought up Patricia and been a foster-mother for many years. It was Tracey who had advised me to get a doctor, and she helped me get antibiotics and soya milk for Rosamund.

We decided to have Rosamund christened during the following July. As she was a much wanted baby, we planned to make this christening into a fairly big event and invited a lot of friends. After the help she'd given us, naturally we asked Tracey and her family to join us. We also planned to surreptitiously repay her the first instalment of the £3,000 we owed her.

Inviting Tracey meant that in turn we received an invitation to Brendon's christening the following October. We accepted, partly because we wanted to see the O'Hallorans again and show them the progress that Rosamund had made. We wanted to see Brendon again, and of course, hand over the next instalment of the money we owed them.

Tracey had advised us to go straight on to the church. I didn't know Flixborough, never having been to this part of Kent before, so we got there very early. Whilst we were waiting outside the church, not quite knowing where to go, an elderly lady came up to us and introduced herself as Tracey's mother. She seemed as outgoing and friendly as Tracey, showed us where to sit and even introduced us to a few other members of Tracey's family.

I was on the phone to Tracey, possibly about the next instalment of money, and happened to mention that we had our call to go out to the Far East again to adopt our second child. Tracey asked me if I anticipated any problems and I said yes. At that time Rosamund still couldn't walk properly and I foresaw difficulties with the pram, because a lot of roads in the Far East are full of holes where heavy rains have pushed up the paving stones, exposing the drains underneath. People connected with the adoption also seemed very nervous about young children being around and kept trying to make you hide the child in your hotel room.

When I mentioned this to Tracey, she promptly suggested that Rosamund go and stay with her whilst we were out of the country. So I took Rosamund down to Flixborough with me to stay for a few days with Tracey so that we could accustom her to those surroundings. When she had settled in, I left to rejoin my husband and travel out to the Far East. Tracey seemed quite capable with the two babies and didn't report any problems when we got back. She remarked that when she'd first seen Rosamund, she could have taken her home, but now of course she and her family had bonded with Brendon. Our second baby was a boy, and we decided to call him Clive.

When Clive was aged about 18 months we received an invitation from the Scottish Circle to attend a celebration of Burns Night, which would be a formal occasion requiring us to wear evening dress and would go on until past midnight. I hadn't been to an evening event since the children had come along and it was something I very much wanted to attend. Again Tracey offered to have both my children come to stay with her for the weekend.

We took the children up there on the Friday, and I also took three evening dresses and had a little 'fashion parade' in front of Tracey. At that time I still didn't know what was really wrong with me, although I knew that I didn't know much about clothes. Tracey helped me choose an evening dress, told me what accessories and shoes to wear and even lent me some jewellery to go with the dress that she had finally chosen.

Here, I must admit, I did unknowingly mislead Tracey. I've always been a very poor speller and tend to write letters backward. I also suffer from figure blindness, which makes all sums very difficult for me. For a long time I thought my trouble was dyslexia. However, having said that, I'd never been tested, partly because all the testing places were way out in the country, charged what to me, at the time, was a lot of money and I had the problem of getting there, and getting someone to look after the children whilst I went there. Finally I thought, well, why bother to get the test done when I know what's wrong? No-one, at that stage, had mentioned the possibility of autism to me, so I started telling people, including Tracey, that I was dyslexic, which I really believed was my trouble. I wish I had been able to get the test done then, just to eliminate it.

When we went to collect the children the following Sunday I noticed that Brendon always made time for both children in his games and actually seemed to have a calming influence on the children. Even Rosamund seemed to get on better with him than she did with Clive. They tended to quarrel less with each other when he was around, too. From then on, I decided to encourage this particular friendship. Michael climbed up to get an old buggy down from his loft, as Rosamund had declared that she was now past the age for twin prams. Michael and Tracey told us that they'd made a video of all the children, but it was decided that it was too late to show us then, so Michael ran us back to the station.

In the early years Rosamund had recurring bouts of sickness. Apparently it can take a foreigner several years to adjust to our climate and food, and with hindsight this was what was wrong with Rosamund. I felt quite concerned about it all and kept trying to ring my mother for her advice, but she never seemed to be there, and always said she would only ever babysit when the children were old enough to go upstairs to the toilet on their own. My mother of course was also very old by this time, and we had never been very close anyway. So I gradually fell into the habit of ringing up Tracey, and she seemed able to offer me some genuine help. In addition to that I was often very lonely in the evenings, because every other week my husband had to work very long hours. Often he wasn't home before one in the morning.

Roughly at this time we were seeing the O'Hallorans about three times a year, once around Christmas, once in the late summer. At her suggestion we made a regular thing of meeting for the children's sake on the anniversary of the day we adopted them, one year at her place, the next year at mine. As the years went past, I became even more desirous of encouraging the children's friendship. Meeting Brendon seemed to do them good and he still, even as he grew older, made time for both children. Patricia sometimes played with them as well. In fact, they all seemed to get on with each other very well.

Tracey could be very generous. She gave our daughter beautiful ear studs for pierced ears and some Indian bangles. She also gave us a huge drum with drumsticks for Clive and a book about Pocahontas, which was then a current film, for Rosamund the following year.

1994 was a rather harrowing year for us. After some trouble with our tenants we decided to re-let our basement flat through an agency, which meant that the little flat downstairs was empty for a long time, depriving us of much needed income. Then we suffered a number of family bereavements, the last of which was at the beginning of 1995. Then unfortunately, my husband became seriously ill and needed to be hospitalised for five long weeks, and at one time I became very worried and concerned that he might lose his life.

So during those turbulent times, when the children were finally in bed, I fell, once again, into the habit of ringing Tracey up. I felt reassured to speak with her because she not only had nursing experience, but seemed very knowledgeable in the areas of unions, compensation and where to go for convalescence.

When Rosamund was about six, both she and Clive went down with chickenpox, and when I told Tracey that I hadn't contracted it as a youngster, she very kindly said that if I did catch it now, the children could go and stay with her for quite a long period. She explained to me that if an adult contracts chickenpox they can become very, very ill. Fortunately I didn't get it.

After his illness, my husband's employers placed him on lighter duties and gave him more time off. As both our children were now in school, he decided to take up singing again. As a family we would attend the music festivals associated with his hobby. Occasionally I saw Tracey at these festivals, because her husband was also in a choir. Sometimes I would find her selling programmes, and other times she would be one of the judges. Whatever she was doing, she was always surrounded by a group of friends. Once I asked people about going to the Kentish musical club, but Tracey was adamant that it was only for people who lived in Kent. Once we met a friend of hers, an Italian clarinettist called Marisa. Tracey told me, rather ruefully, that Marisa was closer to them than they were to her. Once Tracey sent us some mattress covers to help Clive with his asthma, and she also bought me a blue lacy jumper.

At one time I was having some problems with Rosamund (she can be very strong-willed). I mentioned this to Tracey, and once again she offered to have Rosamund go and stay with her. So my daughter went to stay with them for the third time. About a year after that, Tracey offered to have Rosamund go and stay with her again, but this time Rosamund, who was by now a bit older, said she didn't want to go.

We had often discussed a possible return to their country of birth and had 'floated' all sorts of ideas. Perhaps we could go for a year as a member of Oxfam, but that idea was soon shelved. We never made any definite plans as regards exact dates, but we had often spoken about going back, always with the idea of a possible return to the country together. In fact, it was Tracey who had advised me to get in touch with the Nationality Department in order to get our children British passports 'In case we have any trouble getting them back into this country. Do it now,' she said. 'Because there's a two-year waiting list at the moment'. That is what I did, and the children's British passports were duly acquired. This would have been when they were about four, I suppose.

In August, when Rosamund was about seven, I went to see Tracey at her invitation. I took three pairs of roller skates with me, and we took the children up to a local park, helped them get fitted up in them and watched whilst they skated around. They all seemed to have a good time, but whereas formerly I'd always thought that the children got on so well together, I now detected a bit of moodiness in Brendon. When we returned to Tracey's home for our supper I wanted to use the toilet and went upstairs, as the one downstairs was occupied.

As I walked back downstairs, I heard absolute chaos break out between all the children and the adults. The entire household of Tracey, Michael, Patricia, Brendon and even my own two, Rosamund and Clive, seemed to be shouting at the tops of their voices. I could hear Tracey yelling, 'And I won't tolerate this kind of behaviour!' I was completely and utterly bewildered as to what was going on. I suppose with hindsight I should really have sorted out what it was all about, but at the time I thought it was just the children's quarrel and it would simply blow over. Very weak and cowardly of me, I suppose, but if adults get drawn into children's quarrels, it can often mushroom out of all proportion, whereas left to itself, it can blow over in a couple of days. My experiences with Tara taught me that.

I reflected that I considered Tracey to be a very good friend of mine. The children had been to stay with her more than once. In fact, I myself had been to stay with her. We'd met frequently and there had been telephone calls and letters in addition to that. Wouldn't anyone have thought of her as a friend under those circumstances?

Then one day Tracey started talking about going back to the children's country of birth with a group of friends from the Kent Musician's Club. Her plans didn't seem to include me, but at first I didn't say anything, because I knew we couldn't afford it. Then my husband was made redundant with a generous pay-off (he took part of his pension as a payout, which did in fact make it quite large). However, we decided not to spend any of the money until he secured a permanent job.

Now that my husband was at home most evenings, he soon noticed how often I was ringing Tracey. 'I don't want you ringing that woman so often,' he said. 'It's got to stop.' He had never liked her very much anyway. But even he didn't guess what was coming.

My husband did all sorts of jobs at that time. Once he worked in a cemetery, gardening in preparation for its open day. Another time he was in Smithfield Meat market, then at the Guildhall school of music helping to move heavy pianos around. All this continued for some months. Then I suggested to him that he try for a permanent job, this time in the catering business, and he started answering adverts. Once, he was on the verge of being offered a job in a hotel, but it fell through at the last minute. A month later they rang back and asked if by any chance he was still interested, as the man they'd taken on hadn't proved very suitable. So finally he did find a permanent job, even though he had to work a month's trial period first. By the 16th of January 1998, the trial period had been successfully completed and they offered him a permanent position. Now we could start spending his redundancy lump sum. That same day I wrote to Tracey, saying we'd like to be involved in her trip to the country where Rosamund and Clive had been born.

I had been confidently expecting a reply by return of post, saying we would be welcomed and I had been planning to write or phone back and ask her if she would help me with some spring shopping, as I had no idea of what suited me and would have liked to buy some new clothes. But the weeks slipped by and she didn't reply, so I wrote again. This time I sent the letter by registered post. This time she did reply, but didn't refer to what I'd said. This time I thought perhaps I'd better ring her. Then I would definitely know one way or another, and if she didn't want us, then at least we'd know why.

When I phoned that evening her husband Michael answered the telephone, as it seemed that Tracey was staying with relatives in Ireland for a few weeks. Michael said that Tracey would welcome us and gave us details of all the dates and hotels people were staying at. I said to him, 'Are you quite sure that Tracey does actually want us?' He said, 'Yes, quite sure,' and repeated this three times.

So on hearing this, the next day I wrote to the travel agent and booked places for myself and my family. He said it would still be possible to get us all in, although by now things had been left a bit late.

A couple of days later the travel agent phoned us back to say that he hadn't been able to get us in after all, and there appeared to be something he wasn't telling us. But we'd told our children that we were going and as there wasn't much time, we'd even given them their jabs and they had got all excited about it, so we didn't feel that we could back down at this point. So we started e-mailing hotels and got flights and hotels fixed up under our own steam.

The next day I telephoned Tracey, and I thought she would be pleased to learn that we had managed to get in anyway. To my surprise, Tracey started shouting down the phone at me. She now told me that on every occasion when I'd visited her she'd been waiting for me to go. She also said that I was 'alright in small doses', which were the very words my mother used when making fun of my sister Verity behind her back. According to Tracey I had been rude to her mother eight years before at Brendon's christening. The worst thing was that I could now hear real hatred in her voice.

I remembered Brendon's christening very differently. Tracey's mother had tried to draw us in, as she saw that we were on our own. I could remember taking a jigsaw for Patricia so that she wouldn't feel left out, as so much of the attention would have been on Brendon that day. What's more, I had actually seen Patricia doing the jigsaw when I was staying with them. As an autistic woman, I find social occasions very difficult to cope with, so I try to be the one who does the washing up or helps the hostess pass the food around. I expect it was something like this, that Tracey herself, not her mother, objected to. Maybe she must have thought I was trying to take the place over or something?

What Tracey had apparently told the travel agent was that my daughter Rosamund was a spoilt little brat who I didn't have much control over. My husband was also convinced that his race came into it somehow.

When we arrived in the birth country, we made our way to the hotel where the others were staying. We tried to be as pleasant to Tracey and the others as we could, but she still managed to snap at me when she thought nobody else was in earshot. We would not be drawn into a scene as we had to consider the other families who had booked in, and we left thinking that we had managed a potentially difficult situation reasonably well. Tracey took the others on a trip to see some cave paintings, but we joined them at another hotel a few days later. Towards the end of our stay, the waitress started showing us all to the same big dining table. Marisa was there – so much for Tracey saying that she was closer to them than they were to her. Obviously she'd said the same thing to her about us.

Some time after we came back, we received a letter from a niece of Tracey's, saying that she'd heard we'd split up and that she thought that Tracey was still fond of me, and could she do anything to help, perhaps act as a mediator between us? I thought about this and came to the conclusion that Tracey must have regretted our final split and urged her niece to try and make amends. Then I looked at her niece's address and noticed that she didn't live anywhere near either of us, so how did she plan to do it? By letters, e-mails or telephone presumably? Tracey's niece would, in any case, be bound to be biased in her favour. Perhaps if we were given 'counselling', it had better be from someone who was a stranger to us both. So I wrote to Tracey and suggested this, of course without mentioning her niece. But Tracey did not want counselling or indeed any kind of reconciliation.

Then I began to try and unpick exactly what Tracey had told her niece. It was possibly something like, 'I don't see Dulcie anymore. We've had some kind of misunderstanding.' And her niece must have decided to act completely on her own initiative. Then I re-read her niece's letter and thought that perhaps I had just misunderstood it. It is very easy to read what you want into in a letter when you've got a condition such as Asperger's syndrome.

Shocking to me was the fact that Tracey had been prepared to make her own husband lose so much face. If my husband had invited someone to a party, however unintentionally, I'd have just dug in and made the best of it. And if it had been my Mum and Dad, and he'd invited someone unintentionally, and my Mum had then gone to tell them that they weren't welcome, he'd have given her a right old bollocking.

Then I began to wonder if I'd misread the situation entirely and that in fact it was Tracey's husband Michael who hadn't wanted us there? Of course there are plenty of men who like to act 'Mr Nice Guy' and then say to their wives privately, 'Look, I don't like that woman much, get rid of her, will you?'

Trying to find some peace from these raging questions, I decided to go for some counselling myself. I took along the file of Tracey's letters. An old letter of Tracey's happened to catch my eye. It had been written long before our split and in it she said, 'Whilst clearing out my mother's house after her death, I found some old vases and some silk flowers. My mother remembered you from Brendon's christening and I think she would have liked you to have them.' So much for my being rude to her at Brendon's christening. This accusation offended me even more in recalling it now, because even though I may not be able to read body language, take hints and innuendoes as others are able to, I have, however, been told that I have always been well-mannered and courteous. On top of this I am not a confrontational person by any means.

The counsellor looked at the letter and said, 'You will probably never know why this family took you up and then dropped you. But now you know that this woman is a liar, any attempt at reconciliation will only be met by further lies. And even if you do manage to scrape some form of friendship together again, how do you know she won't do something similar in the future? Could you ever trust this person again?'

I suppose I must have been a bit of a dope, because at this stage I still thought that our respective children actually liked each other. I just couldn't get out of my head how well they all seemed to get along. After that, whenever our paths crossed with the Kent musicians, I would often ask Rosamund and Clive to go over and try to talk to Brendon when we saw him.

When Rosamund was 10, we gave her a sleepover party and issued a general invitation to all the youngsters in the Kent young musicians club, rather hoping that Brendon would come. Not only did he not come, but Tracey organised a sleepover on the same day (we'd adopted together, so his birthday was only two days before Rosamund's). It felt to me at the time that this 'coincidence' was planned deliberately to try and ruin Rosamund's party. Now I began to see the real woman behind the friendly facade she had always presented. So much for her supposedly 'liking' Rosamund.

One night shortly after that, while I was putting the children to bed, I heard them say their prayers and was just about to put their lights out when Rosamund said, 'Why doesn't Auntie Tracey like us any more?' I thought about it for a minute and then told her the whole sorry tale about how Tracey had tried to ruin her party, and the other things she'd done. I felt my daughter was asking me for the truth, and so I needed to tell her the whole truth. Rosamund didn't say anything, but when I passed her room the next day I noticed that the Pocahontas book, the Indian bangles and even the little gold cross and chain that Tracey had given Rosamund on the occasion of her christening were all in the waste paper basket.

A couple of years later, I found out something that I wished I'd known about long before. When they were in the birth country, Brendon had told my children that he no longer wished to be their friend. Thus inviting him (even in the general way I did) to Rosamund's party had been a complete waste of time. So it is possible that either he, or Patricia, may have had a hand in the final split up. Now I began to realise that there must have been a lot more in the chaotic quarrel I had partly witnessed the day I went up there with the skates. Perhaps I should really date our breakup from then.

A short time after this, I received a letter from Tracey that just about tied everything up. In it she said she'd always found our friendship a burden right from the very first day, and she'd only ever been friendly with us because firstly, they wanted their money back, and secondly because she'd thought that I couldn't cope with Rosamund. She'd only waited until my husband was better and the chickenpox scare was over, and then she'd just been waiting for the opportunity to engineer some kind of quarrel.

With hindsight, I should never have let Rosamund go and stay with Tracey. But she had offered, and I hadn't known. I now realise that Tracey would be alright with any suggestion that comes from her, such as 'See you on Sunday,' 'Have lunch now,' 'Go for a walk down this lane,' and so on. Most of the time it works, people are in holiday mood and are happy to fall in with whatever she suggests. But then one day we clashed over a principle. That's why she wouldn't agree to counselling: because the suggestion came from me, not her.

I realise that my having Asperger's Syndrome is likely to place a very heavy burden on any relationship. I also know that the true extent of my condition is not immediately apparent and that sometimes, after people have got to know me, they pull away in defeat. I suppose for a lot of people, I have been one of their 'worthy causes', as they had hoped, on meeting me, to perhaps point me in the right direction, or change me in some way for the better. This is the fundamental problem with a condition such as Asperger's: it is not something you can ever 'iron out'. If I could have told her what was really wrong with me, right at the very beginning, would it have made a difference? Maybe not. People always say, 'Tell them, and then they can make allowances for you,' although they hardly ever do. Some people say that they could tell about 20 minutes after meeting me that there was something wrong with me. Tracey, apparently, put it all down to immaturity.

I know that there's no power on earth that can make any one like you if they don't, but I can't say that we were really happy about the way she chose to end the relationship. I think that in retrospect, it would have been much better if she could have ended it all when the children were about two. Then they wouldn't be able to remember, neither her nor Brendon. Failing that, she could have hung on until they were about 14. Then they could have e-mailed each other if they wanted to, or even arranged to meet somewhere in London. The way it was done has just left everything hanging. All she had to do was tell her friends on the trip to the birth country that I was recovering from a nervous breakdown, or something, for why I was inclined to be a bit clingy. One family even told us that they'd never even seen Tracey before. So she preferred people that she'd never even seen before to people like us, who had known her so long. One more rejection for me, who has already faced so many and a little bit further for my confidence to slip.

Since the split with Tracey I have joined an art class, which I found very therapeutic, and a reading circle. I've also been tracing my ancestors and writing down the dates of the births, marriages and deaths of the long dead, and that has had an immensely calming effect on me. As a family, we've been camping in France and Italy, and we've visited Iceland and Australia, so I've put some kind of life back together again.

The humiliating and painful rift with Tracey's family represented the last straw in a long line of incomprehensible rejections that finally prompted me to seek professional help and an eventual diagnosis. It was perhaps mainly because I saw my children suffer in the aftermath, especially my daughter, that I found within myself a new steely determination to find out exactly what was wrong with me. My life had been awash with the 'nature or nurture' hypothesis. I knew myself that I displayed characteristics that belonged to both categories, such as a form of dyslexia, clumsiness, overheating, obsessional repetitive behaviour and poor social awareness.

Second guessing, as I had done with the supposed dyslexia, would not be good enough now. Before, I had told people what I 'thought' I had. Now I was compelled to find out exactly what it was. I was referred to various doctors before I eventually saw a senior psychiatrist who noted my symptoms as possibly being within the range of autism. He then referred me to a renowned expert in the field of autism. I waited some considerate time to see this expert, as people were referred to her from all over the country.

When I was finally seen by this specialist psychiatrist in her consulting room she told me afterwards that she had realised what I was suffering from very early on in the meeting. In order to assess me, I was asked to fill in a long questionnaire, where I was asked for my views on lots of unrelated things. For the first time ever, I was not grilled about my childhood experiences, but was actually asked what I 'thought' about things. My answers to the questionnaire proved to be completely typical of someone with Asperger's, and she informed me that no further tests would be required.

The specialist psychiatrist was very kind to me and said she regretted that I had 'slipped through the system', and that most resources are poured into detecting children with it. She remarked that my parents must have had their suspicions, but of course that was a long time ago. She also commented that I fell within the small group within the group of Asperger sufferers that were married. She explained to me that there was no cure or medication that would help me, and that Obsessive Compulsive Disorder can mask the autism for a long time. She gave me guidelines about how to manage my daily 'rituals', and since then I have developed a new 'intellectual' awareness of myself that most people understand about themselves instinctively from birth. This helps my poor self-awareness. In that way, I superimpose intellect where 'instinct' is lacking. My close relationships have improved considerably since my diagnosis, and I now feel able to ask people to help me more in trying to understand others. I also now understand a major part of the daily frustration I used to feel with the world around me, and as a result I feel more at peace with myself.

A couple of years before our final split, Tracey gave me a long length of curtain material that I used it to make into four attractive little curtains. I hung up the supporting baton myself and made the little contrasting hems on them. Whilst I was doing them I often thought of the day when I would proudly show them to Tracey and say, 'Look what I made of the curtain material that you gave me'. Shortly after the split, I looked at them again and realised that now, she will never see them. We moved away from that house about eight years ago, and of course we will never see the video that they took of our children (that is, if they haven't destroyed it), and a wave of inexplicable sadness suddenly swept over me, although I realise that there is nothing anybody can do about it now.

CHAPTER TWENTY-ONE
Living and Coping

Asperger's Syndrome is a condition which winds itself so deeply into the human personality that it's impossible to know where the condition begins, and where selfhood ends. Every single sufferer can experience a completely different range of symptoms. So I thought I would just give a checklist for parents and children. I have listed the symptoms in the order they first appeared in me, but I've had to rely on an extremely fallible human memory, and on what I was told about myself from my parents and friends.

I'm told I had an <u>accelerated growth rate</u>, sitting up, walking and passing all my milestones early. Autistic children can also lag behind others and seem slow.

Apparently I went through a period of '<u>echo talking</u>', repeating everything my mother said. Suddenly, when I was about three years old, for to apparent reason I started talking and answering questions normally.

I was always very <u>clumsy</u>. My mother told me that I was the one who broke all the cut glass vases that she had been given as wedding presents. I fell out of a high chair, went over in the garden rockery, had a nursing chair fold up on me and was always falling over.

At two years old I was brought home in a police car having been found sitting on a little stall outside the local station watching the trains go by. Always prone to <u>wandering away</u> it was made worse by the fact that I couldn't tell the difference between right and left and was always getting lost.

<u>I didn't really have a sense of any kind of danger</u>. At about three I tried to get some dolls' clothes out of a

copper of boiling water and badly scalded myself in the process. I heard about another child whose parents decided one wintry day to take a walk along the banks of a frozen canal, when suddenly the child ran down onto the untested ice.

At nursery school the teachers asked my parents to stop bringing a <u>favourite doll</u> to school, as I seemed to be under the impression that it was a real person. A refusal to be parted from a favourite toy is a symptom of Asperger's.

Still <u>clumsy</u> at school, I was the one who fell out of a tree in the school playground, fell off the rope in the playground and fell (twice) from the climbing horse in the gymnasium. All this got so bad that the school suggested that my parents get my sight checked. Then they wondered if I was wearing 'slippery' shoes.

My clumsiness, plus the fact that I <u>wrote letters backwards</u> and covered my work with large ink blobs, led people to wonder if I could possibly be dyslexic.

When I was about seven I can remember <u>crying for hours</u> because nobody had heard me say my prayers.

I was always prone to <u>sleeplessness</u> and was continually yawning at school. The teachers suggested that my parents put me to bed earlier.

As I grew older the crying fits became <u>giggling attacks</u>, <u>laughing</u> at things other people didn't think were funny, or even prolonged <u>hiccupping</u> or <u>coughing attacks</u>. These attacks have one thing in common: the sufferer cannot stop.

I became <u>very cold</u> in winter and was always catching colds. Of course I had the opposite problem in summer and <u>overheated with excessive sweating</u> and tended to start stripping off. The salts in my sweat led to a skin eruption, and I also suffered from excessive thirst. This can lead to Asperger's being mistaken for other conditions, like diabetes.

It sometimes seems as if the body, aware of the great difficulty the sufferer labours under, <u>overdevelops other senses</u> to try and compensate. I developed an unusually acute sense of hearing, making the sleeplessness worse. At one time I could overhear private conversations from the next house. And I have an <u>unusually good memory</u>. In this respect Asperger's differs from other mental illnesses that can lead to great blanks in the memory. An unusually <u>strong sense of smell (and taste)</u> is a possibility too.

Again it seems as if nature is trying to make up for the enormous disability that the person suffers by making the child <u>unusually good looking</u>, or even <u>beautiful</u>. This didn't happen in my case.

The lack of a sense of danger continued, and as I became a teenager I didn't see the dangers of going up and talking to strange men.

The child may develop some kind of <u>obsession</u>. With me it was trains and railway timetables. Even today I go everywhere by train.

I tended to live in a kind of bubble. I'm told I was 'oblivious to other people' and seemed to 'live in a dream world,' was 'always half asleep' or 'not quite with it'. Others more kind said that I seemed to be 'always lost in thought' or, more unkindly, 'dense' or 'thick' or even 'looked as if you are carrying the troubles of the whole world on your shoulders'. This can be mistaken for deafness, selfishness or even rudeness.

I also suffered from <u>shaking hands</u>, and this made me slow at school when it came to things like catching the ball. If I shook hands people would say, 'Just what are you afraid of?'

I <u>couldn't understand</u> what was meant by '<u>body language</u>': take hints, see jokes, or even know when someone is joking, or work out idioms.

The lack of understanding between yourself and other people can lead to it being <u>impossible to</u> <u>make friends</u>. The sufferer can also be <u>targeted by bullies</u>. As an adult you can be targeted by some extreme religious or a militant political group who can use you as a pawn. You go along with all their thinking because you want to belong so much. There is, too, another kind of exploitation, particularly if you are one of the Asperger 'good lookers'. You can be targeted by a man who simply wants an affair. A number of Asperger people end up with children and no spouse. Another horrifying example is the man who simply wants an affair, then drops you, and you finish up by becoming a stalker.

Unable to make friends I became an avid reader. I've read all Jane Austen's works, all the Brontë sisters plus a number of George Eliot's and Anthony Trollope's, and most of the novels by Charles Dickens. My first husband, who taught literature, said he'd never known anyone who'd read as much as I had. I have read over 400 books concerning the Second World War.

The sufferer likes to <u>have a routine</u> and stick to it. The 'favourite toy' of childhood now becomes a favourite piece of furniture or picture that always has to hang in the same place. In my first house, for example, I painted every single room and ceiling white.

The sufferer may be prone to <u>exaggeration</u>. For example, a man putting his arm round you could be seen as rape. Or, conversely, a man who is just plain kind may be seen as 'interested'. This could lead to a sufferer hanging round a man who isn't really keen on them. Seeing things as exaggerations can lead to your being called a 'liar' or a 'troublemaker'.

If the sufferer is a woman, she may have an <u>extremely 'colourful' imagination</u>, have vivid dreams, or possibly paint in bright colours or embroider in 'loud' colours, or dress in contrasting colours. This can lead to one being mistaken for, say, a gypsy. The intense earnestness of one's personality may lead to the sufferer being mistaken for someone of another nationality, particularly if they <u>use words in a different way</u> to other people, otherwise known as 'atypical use of language'.

The sufferer may <u>shy away from physical contact</u>. This could lead a social worker to wonder if a child has been abused.

The sufferer may <u>not speak</u> for a long time or be <u>very quiet</u>. I was always very <u>voluble</u>, but tended to slur my words. I'm told that people thought that I took drugs. The sufferer will probably be bad at all games where a steady hand is called for, like archery or darts, but be good at something like football, which really calls for speed and strength.

If female, the child may be good at anything which calls for imagination, like essay writing, but very bad at anything which calls for figure work, like mathematics or even anatomy and physiology. The opposite may happen if the child is male. I was never able to learn to drive a car.

The child may be very 'faddy' in food and this can even develop into a full-blown anorexia nervosa.

The lack of insight into other people's reactions can lead to one being accused of 'chasing people', because they have misinterpreted what you've seen as a friendly remark. You can also be accused of 'nosiness' or even 'crawling'. The song 'What Do You Want To Make Those Eyes At Me For, If They Don't Mean What They Say' could well apply to me, as I simply could not see myself as others saw me. My shyness was mistaken for aloofness, and I tended to cover my timidity with aggression.

Some people may be annoyed by the mood swings and strange behaviour in the sufferer. Others may simply avoid you because you can't cope with it, but others may find it a bit funny. As you get older, your odd speech rhythms and perhaps slightly eccentric behaviour, particularly if you keep forgetting things and losing them, lead to the condition being mistaken for the onset of dementia. A sufferer will also repeat themselves often, and this too can be mistaken for early onset dementia.

Not all symptoms may be present and not all in that order. I am still building up my database, but I think that what I have written above, as I remember it, just about sums it up.

Coping:

Never try and self-diagnose. Don't waste everybody's time by going to see any kind of psychotherapist. You need to see a properly qualified psychiatrist, preferably one who is a neurologist and properly equipped to cope with someone with learning difficulties. When properly assessed (and this may take some time) don't waste time with a therapist. It will only cost you or the country a lot of time and money and they can't do anything. In this country, anyone can set themselves up as some kind of therapist without any kind of training at all. Most psychotherapists have an arts degree and some kind of course in elementary psychology. Don't waste your time, money or even the country's money.

In recent years a few support groups have sprung up especially for Asperger people, with therapists especially trained to deal solely with Asperger people. I haven't tried any of these out, but my own experience would suggest that they can't really do all that much. There is no cure and pills are consequently useless.

Because Asperger people can be targeted by bullies and find it so difficult to make friends, they can very possibly tell a therapist that it seems to them as if everybody has it in for them. This can lead to the condition being mistaken for paranoid schizophrenia, which can lead to incarceration in a hospital and even dangerous drugs. There are plenty of horror stories around about Asperger victims in mental hospitals. Of course patients are prone to exaggerate, but some of it must be true.

On a social level, try and avoid occasions which are purely social and go to something where you have something to do, like handing out the food. It's also helpful to join structured groups, like a political meeting or a Bible study group or art class, as opposed to a group of people meeting for just 'chatting'. If you do go to a party, try to help with the washing up, or ask if you can be the one who helps the hostess pass round the cakes. You will tend to be happier when you actually have something to do rather than go to a purely social occasion.

There are particular problems associated with marriage, as the other person will be carrying a heavy burden and will need a lot of help. In addition to the difficulties of living with someone who is mentally ill, the other person may have to shoulder some of the financial burdens, too. With cutbacks at every turn, Asperger people could find it very difficult to get jobs. It could also take you longer to pick up a job than other people. The epithet 'Last to be hired and first to be fired' could well apply to you. I suppose my own advice would be to try and become self-employed, or possibly do a job where you're working on your own a lot.

One of the difficulties in marriage is that a happy marriage is full of compromises, which help to keep a mind flexible. This flexibility of mind is something that an Asperger person will find very difficult to maintain. Try to explain to a spouse that to you, the world doesn't really make sense and to make it make sense you may find it easier if every piece of furniture stays in the same place, or have every room painted the same colour, and that moving (no matter how large your family has grown) is something you'll probably find very traumatic.

There is another problem with children. The frustrations of being an Asperger person (not the condition itself) can result in someone (particularly men) falling into a blind rage. Children will find this very difficult to tolerate and they may be puzzled by your mood swings. The only thing I can suggest is to get yourself correctly diagnosed and, as soon as they are old enough, tell them. Hopefully, when they themselves become adults, they can understand.

Your best bet (I think) is to tell people that there's something wrong and try to explain what it is. Most people have a picture of mental illness in their minds of someone going berserk and running around with a knife or something, and they are prone to call out, 'What? You've broken another cup? Can't you learn to take greater care?' Once, when I kept crashing into things, someone asked me if I had a lesion in the brain. My own husband said that the number of things I've spilt or broken is the thing about my condition that he finds the hardest of all to cope with.

Had my condition been caught as a child they could have dealt with the clumsiness. It's too late now. I am an adult and my clumsiness will never go.

My own way of dealing with the clumsiness is to try and make as much space around myself as possible. Dispense with things like room dividers and perpendicular 'breakfast bars' in the kitchen. In the garden, try and create an open lawn as opposed to a patio/tiled-type garden. Then if you do go over, you won't hurt yourself so much. In the kitchen and drawing room, try and get ornaments etc. into enclosed glass cupboards which lock (don't lose the key), and place everything, even little coffee tables, against the walls. This will help to prevent you from continually barging into things or breaking things whenever you do the dusting. However, it won't cure you.

As regards feelings of excessive heat or cold, I find its best to avoid anything made of nylon or Crimplene, particularly blouses or underwear. Wear lace-up shoes to help prevent yourself from repeatedly tripping over. In winter I try to wear wool and I personally find something with a so-called 'classical' or round neck with a cotton blouse with an overhanging collar the most comfortable.

I find wool the warmest, particularly something hand knitted. Knitting makes wonderful therapy, too.

Not knowing the difference between left and right is more difficult. If you wear a wedding or engagement ring, try to get one with an 'L' on it and just glance at your hand when you give or receive directions.

In order to cope with sleeplessness, try and have your main meal at midday rather than in the evening, and watch your diet carefully. Have no more than four cups of tea or coffee a day and, if possible, never after 5pm. If you are a man, don't be tempted to drink, it will only ensure that you will have drinking problems, too.

Hopefully you will find some of the above helpful.

Bibliography – Some of this was Helpful to me

General books about Mental Health

1. 'The Lost Days of My Life', Jane Simpson (pub. Pan 1958)

2. 'Will There Really Be A Morning', Frances Farmer (pub. Dell 1974)

3. 'An Angel At My Table', Janet Frame (pub. Women's Press 2001)

4. 'The Lobotomist', Jack El-Hai (pub. Wiley 2007)

5. 'History of Psychiatry', Edward Shorter (pub. Wiley 1998)

These books have some terrible events recorded in them and partly explain my parents' distrust of psychiatrists.

Books that deal specifically with autism

1. 'Fugitive Mind', Peter Rowlands (pub. Littlehampton 1979)

2. 'For The Love Of Ann', James Copeland (pub. Ballantine 1976)

3. 'George and Sam: Autism In The Family', Charlotte Moore (pub. St Martin's 2006)

4. 'Emergence: Labelled Autistic', Temple Grandin (pub. Warner 1996)

Lightning Source UK Ltd.
Milton Keynes UK
UKOW040041210613

212606UK00001B/1/P